Dancing with Dynamite
By Tim Huff

Dancing
with Dynamite

celebrating against the odds

Tim Huff

Foreword by Jean Vanier

Benediction by Sue Mosteller, C.S.J.

CASTLE QUAY BOOKS

Dancing With Dynamite: Celebrating Against the Odds
Copyright ©2010 Tim Huff
All rights reserved
Printed in Canada
International Standard Book Number: 978-1-894860-49-9

Published by:
Castle Quay Books
1307 Wharf Street, Pickering, Ontario, L1W 1A5
Tel: (416) 573-3249
E-mail: info@castlequaybooks.com
www.castlequaybooks.com

All illustrations by Tim Huff
Copy edited by Janet Dimond
Cover design by THINKHOUSE COMMUNICATION DESIGN
Printed at Essence Publishing, Belleville, Ontario

Library and Archives Canada Cataloguing in Publication

Huff, Tim, 1964-
    Dancing with dynamite : celebrating against the
odds / Tim Huff ; foreword by Jean Vanier ; benediction
by Sue Mosteller.

Includes bibliographical references.
ISBN 978-1-894860-49-9

    1. Social problems. 2. Social advocacy. 3. Social acceptance.
4. Compassion. 5. Kindness. 6. Hope Exchange (Toronto, Ont.).
7. Huff, Tim, 1964-. I. Title.

HN110.T6H83 2010   362'.042   C2010-906163-2

CASTLE QUAY BOOKS

Contents

Author's Acknowledgements

Having created author's acknowledgements sections twice before (for two previous Castle Quay Books releases), I have come to recognize three very pertinent matters. First—as far as I'm concerned, this is the most difficult part of the book to write. Second—these sections are akin to a time capsule, one that identifies relationships, new and old, as they stand in the moment. This is both a very complex and intriguing matter. Third—just as I ponder in one of this book's chapters, for everything there is seemingly a proverbial "line in the sand" that must be drawn. To that end, for this book I have entered into this section of thanksgiving needing to draw that line at people who have inspired and encouraged me directly regarding, and for, this book project and over the season it unfolded. The list of those I love and admire surely transcends this.

There is no greater gift than the opportunity to thrive in a household of love and laughter. To my lovely wife, Diane, and my awesome children, Sarah Jane and Jake—you are complete joy to me and cherished endlessly.

My earnest thanks to Larry Willard at Castle Quay Books Canada, not just for being an excellent publisher, but for being a true gentleman and a true friend. My heartfelt thanks to Janet Dimond, for both her professionalism and thoughtfulness with all of the material as the book's editor and for her kind encouragement to me. Likewise to Marina Hoffman at Castle Quay Books Canada for her hard work and support.

As always, a very special thanks to my dear friend and associate Julia Beazley, for her excellent work, creativity and faithfulness to a myriad of ongoing endeavours and the entire *Dancing With Dynamite* project. And most of all—for her wonderful friendship.

There are no words that do justice to what's felt when Jean Vanier's words grace your book. And that they do so generously is simply and outright overwhelming. Jean, I am so humbled.

Author's Acknowledgements

The only honour grander than having the sweet words of Sister Sue Mosteller shared as your benediction is knowing her as a sacred friend, advisor and confidante. Thank you, my very dear friend.

Once again, my very humble thanks to Terri and Miller Alloway and family and the Maranatha Foundation and Lightworks, for standing with me and supporting me in so many ways, professionally and personally—and always so thoughtfully—over many years and throughout many projects, including the writing and release of this book.

I could write on and on about how much Lori and John McAuley's friendship and support have meant to me personally and to my entire family. Individually, and as a couple, Lori and John have blessed me with unlimited friendship, care and grace. "Thank you" is far from enough.

My deepest gratitude to Debbie and Don Morrison for sharing incredible measures of generosity by way of support, hospitality, counsel, encouragement, laughter and friendship.

Great thanks to my dear friends Joanne and Gary Scullion for all the ways you have shared your kindness, enthusiasm and imagination for new and exciting things to come.

To Laura Jane and Gord Brew: Together you (and Thinkhouse Design) are a creative force that is unmatched, and individually you are uniquely to be celebrated. And that I do. Thank you for the countless ways you stay with me.

I would be remiss not to mention my great thanksgiving for the kindness, friendship and generosity of The Honourable Hilary M. Weston over a great many years. Such an honour.

Always, I'm so thankful for the many years of excellent leadership and visioning I have known serving with John Wilkinson, the executive director of Youth Unlimited (Toronto YFC). Beyond that great honour, John and Trish have also been faithful and dear friends and encouragers.

Along with the aforementioned Lori McAuley, Sister Sue Mosteller and John Wilkinson, five others round out an eight-person group that faithfully stands by me as a personal wellness and advocacy team—praying for me, listening to me, advising me and graciously cheering me on. These extraordinary brothers and sisters are Steve Bell, Annie Brandner, Alan Davey, Sharon Gernon and Greg Paul. I'm endlessly thankful to, and for, each one.

To my mom and dad (Arlene and Liv)—I never get over wanting to make you proud of me, because I'm always so proud of you. Likewise, I'm blessed with the love and support of my brothers (Liv Jr. and Dan) and their very dear families, as well as Diane's family (Keith Johnson, Linda Revie and the boys, and Barbara Ward and kids).

It's an anxious thing to allow your raw written words into the hands of others at any time, but even more so just as you are first processing them. The sounding board provided by these exceptional friends as they received first drafts of the unedited manuscript was vital for me. To these people, whom I trust implicitly, admire and love, know that each of you is so uniquely and greatly appreciated by me: Cheryl Bear-Barnetson and Randy Barnetson, Nanci Bell, Karen Clausen-Dockrill, Cathy Dienesch, Michael Frost, Adrienne Grant, Alan Hirsch, Mike and Jodi Janzen, Sarah Lester, Angela Porter, Bill and Shanan Rice, Sherri Spence and Brenda Tennant.

It's not simple, especially in a book that is ultimately about coming together, to succinctly list the communities that have shaped me personally. Any and all that you find mentioned in the chapters you read have my utmost respect and admiration. But again, there are special communities filled with very personal friendships that are impossible for me to miss mentioning here: Bob Rumball Associations for the Deaf, Daily Bread Food Bank, Frontlines, Hockey for the Homeless, Impact Romania, L'Arche Daybreak, the National Roundtable on Poverty and Homelessness and the many Street Level agencies and associates across Canada, Weston Park Baptist Church, World Vision, and YFC chapters across Canada, the US and worldwide.

Thank you to the incredibly devoted Light Patrol staff and volunteer team, the entire Youth Unlimited (Toronto YFC) staff and board, as well as the many supporters—individuals, families, churches and businesses—who have stood with me in countless ways for so many years.

One of the great honours that has been mine has been to share in bridging partnerships that some people would not anticipate. The Muskoka Woods leadership team and staff have been an extraordinary encouragement and inspiration to me and my entire family, and to many of my co-workers and colleagues. A wonderful gift!

It is virtually impossible to travel the road I have chosen (or found myself wandering on) without the refuge of supportive voices. Thank you to those who very specifically and faithfully chose to encourage me during the hectic season of my life running parallel to the writing of this book: Brett Andrews, Keith Bagg, Tina and Mike Barlow, Cynthia Barlow-Odorizzi, Sue and Dave Bolender, Paul Brandner, Carol Brown, John Cassells, Karen Chambers, Dale Cheslock, Colleen Clarke, Lydia Clinton, David Collison, Alison Cooper, Natalie Davey, Rebecca Davey, Marianne Deeks, Jocelyn Durston, Andrea Earl, Teres Edmonds,

AUTHOR'S ACKNOWLEDGEMENTS

Cheryl and John Frogley-Rawson, Mieke and Dave Geldart, Kristy Grisdale-Opoku, Sandra Groves, Bob and Jan Fukumoto, Pamela and Brian Hanford, Mel Hems, Suzi Higgins, Julie and Steve Hill, Denise Holland, Lori Holtam-Weedon, Annette Jones, Sue and Mark Kocaurek, Clark Kostik, Andy Levy and my friends at Mastermind Educational, Jennine and Bruce Loewen, Gail and Bill Masson, Ron Melanson, Sarah McKenzie, Dawn Curnew-Millar, John Mohan, Allison and Jacob Moon, Carl Nash, Pat Nixon, Scott Oake, Madolyn and Mark Osborne, Dion Oxford, Dorothy Patterson, Shannon Peck, Pauline and Ron Peneycad, Heather Ploeg, Gino Reda, Paul Robertson, Mary-Jean and Bob Rumball, Shelley and Derek Rumball, Diana Schwenk, Fay and Don Simmonds, Ingrid Smith, Iona and Rob Snair, Scott Snider, Glen Soderholm, Carolyn Solby, Rick Tobias, Lori Ward, Donna-Lee and John Waymann, Haidee and David White, Linda Wisz, Collette and Lino Zecca, and my band buddies in Outrider (Pete Bowman, Steve Kennedy and John Russell).

Finally, this book is dedicated to the unlikely heroes you will meet in it—the ones known as "outcasts" who are this world's truest hopegivers. The vocational hopegivers who remain faithful. The strangers who bless by simply being present. Those whose sweet stories are all but lost, but whose tiny portion revealed is sacred. Those who bravely share portions of their stories as a gift and a signpost toward hope and newness. All of these who, just like you, are surely meant to be celebrated. And they are.

Foreword by Jean Vanier

This is a beautiful book about meetings. Tim Huff offers us real-life stories: meetings with young people robbed of the experience of "home"; others caught up in the drugs and harsh realities of street life; and people living in group homes or large institutional settings, many of whom are hurting and cast out. He also describes beautiful meetings with ordinary people. Tim has penetrating, insightful vision, so that he sees people through the eyes of God. He sees goodness and hidden beauty in every person. No fears—only love and an immense hope inspire him.

This is a book of hope and healing. Its author is one man working together with others, to help many brothers and sisters discover their value and inner beauty and move forward in life with renewed hope. Tim is also a man of fun, art and music, who plays in a band that cheers people up and incites others to dance and still others to sing amid the wonder and the pain of life's journey.

A man who does beautiful things, Tim attracts others to do beautiful things. His love is contagious. Instead of gangs and people groups closed in upon themselves, seeking to reveal their power through cruelty and destruction, Tim's heart is to help create open communities where people come together freely to love and give support to each other, and so to bring hope, courage and life to those crying out in need.

This book should be read by young and old alike. Young people may discover new and deeper reasons for living and for true compassion that gives life to others. Older people will be reminded that our society is not only a place of rivalry and competition, but also a network where love is manifested and where hope is born.

Jean Vanier

For nearly four decades, Jean Vanier has travelled the world, fashioning a network of homes where people with developmental disabili-

11

ties, volunteers and staff live together in community. Those we lock away and think worthless, he says, have the power to teach and even to heal us. After attaining a doctorate in philosophy and theology at the Institut Catholique in Paris, Jean chose to forgo career and stature and returned to France, to live in Trosly-Breuil, in community with people with intellectual disabilities. He bought a small house and named it "L'Arche," the French word for Noah's Ark.

As Jean began to give conferences and retreats around the world, the vision of L'Arche spread. In 1969, the first L'Arche Community in North America was founded. In 1981, after handing over the leadership of the International Federation of L'Arche Communities, Jean began to travel the world as its founder, encouraging L'Arche communities and giving spiritual accompaniment and guidance to the many people who came to him from within and beyond L'Arche.

Jean Vanier has received numerous awards, including the French Legion of Honour, Companion of the Order of Canada, the Rabbi Gunther Plaut Humanitarian Award (2001) and the Chicago Catholic Theological Union Blessed are the Peacemakers Award (2006). He continues to travel the world to give retreats and conferences, and to write. His books have been translated into 29 languages. Today, Jean still lives in the first L'Arche community in Trosly-Breuil, France.

Prologue Give Up

Junior high was not good for me. Especially grade 7. That was just plain brutal. I know I stand among a great many when I say so, but at the time I felt like I was definitely in the minority. From my vantage point, it appeared very clear that some kids found their early groove as "cool" around age 12. Others took enormous physical and developmental leaps toward young adulthood in a matter of months. And others just seemed comfortable in their own skin, taking the next small steps in—or toward—puberty in stride.

I did none of these.

But where I was sheepish and cowardly at one end, I was opportunistic at the other—an unsettling combination of attributes that led to the creation of disconcerting memories that last for life.

Unwittingly, via proximity to an elementary school pal who radically changed personas between there and middle school, I one day found myself walking along the Humber River in the west end of Toronto with "the cool kids." They were cursing and smoking cigarettes like the cool kids would, and I was walking a pace behind, fake laughing and agreeing with everything they said like the uncoolest kid imaginable, all the while hoping no one who knew my mom would see me with them.

Just where the river walkway ended was a bench. About a 15-minute, three-and-a-half-cigarette walk from where we'd started. As we neared the bench, I recognized a friend of mine sitting all alone. Just as I was about to leave the pack to greet him, one of the cool kids gestured at him and laughed, as though speaking to another of the cool kids, but loud enough that my friend on the bench was sure to hear.

"What a freak."

I didn't break from the crowd. I didn't speak up. I didn't even look at my sad friend on the bench. I couldn't bear it. I just kept walking with the cool kids. My heart feels as sick about it today as it did more than three decades ago. Indeed, because I was a coward. And that I surely increased the irreversible hurt to my friend. But as much as anything else, because I knew I was no less a freak.

A far cry between circus sideshow fare and a lonely boy on a bench, it seems the gauge on these matters is controlled by those who simply deem themselves worthy. And there's no shortage of them. So I wonder—forced to navigate through a world teeming with oppressors and cowards...where do the freaks belong?

Maybe that's too harsh for you. Maybe not. At least not out loud. Then how about a softer version of the same question, that references misfits or outcasts? How about the uncool kids just sitting alone on a park bench getting teased by the cool kids and ignored by their friends? Whoever, whatever, and by whatever extremes you might gauge them, where do they belong? With you? With me? Someone else perhaps.

Or maybe, of all places imagined, in God's Kingdom?

Most of us, thinking we have our wits reasonably about us on our best days, have a hard enough time trying to figure out where we truly belong ourselves. How on earth can we sort out the rest?

But sooner or later, we all have to give action, voice, or at least a thumbs up or down to a world that technology makes smaller by the day around issues of justice and mercy. If not to the global powers that be, in the least by way of community engagement within our grocery stores, auto shops and little league teams. And doing so won't likely be with speeches and rallies but revealed most vividly in the smallest of our mannerisms. Many of our children have learned more from rolling eyes, long sighs and sarcastic tones than they ever will from outright words.

And so, and still, what about the freaks, outcasts and misfits? What about the losers and lost causes? Even those who exist in yet another realm, less slighted by name calling, but still dwelling outside of "normal"—known in worldly terms as the unfortunate, the ill-fated, and the unlucky? In the grand scheme, the true master plan, where do any of them fit into God's blueprint?

If that's not enough, let's take it even further. Not simply those who are inexplicably endearing in their special needs or requiring a bit of extra attention. Not just the ones who need a tearful second chance or a friendly season of life-skills training. We allow these ones to vie for poster-child positions for any number of charities, almost purposeful in their plight. Someone sweet needs a kidney. Someone can't see, but still smiles.

Someone frail is fighting booze. Someone adorable is born lacking. Someone a million miles away starves and suffers beneath the relentless desert sun. On and on it goes—if we let it—until we're numb. Or, for a great many, until we change the channel.

But what about really looking at the big picture? Way beyond sad slogans and puppy dog eyes. Where do the real "others" belong? The hodgepodge of unluckies, outsiders and oddities that the Western world has historically and viciously categorized and systematically rubber-stamped, by circumstance, optics and assumption, is mind-boggling! A dubious gaggle of unfortunates painted with social descriptors only decades ago that have since yielded to a *status quo* public sensitivity and political correctness, but that remain spoken of no less today under breath at cocktail parties and water coolers, and boisterously in high school halls and billiard parlours. The profane, cruel, heretical and biblical—mixed and matched by untidy reference and street slang like odd socks coming out of the laundry. Winos and drunks. Orphans and bastards. Retards and mutants. Schizos. Whores. Degenerates. Crackheads. Indigents. Low-lifes. The lost. The lame. The lacking. The needy. The cursed. The damned.

What glorious Kingdom of God includes all of these? Is it all simply a paranormal scam? A supernatural prank?

While I surrendered any notion of formal theological studies in my young adulthood to wide-eyed interest in rock music, creative arts and motor sports, I still believe the eternal truths of God's Kingdom are meant to be available to one such as me as much as anyone else, by the virtues of simple faith and authentic seeking. If this is so, then to ponder "the Kingdom of God" takes no more nudge than recalling a daily exercise from childhood.

Of all the things that North American baby boomers learned, one that fails few memories, believers and non alike, is the Lord's Prayer. Straight from the New Testament. Part of the once-upon-a-time elementary school system routine, day in and day out. In it, the first thing out of the gate, past addressing God and His holiness, is "Thy kingdom come, Thy will be done in earth, as it is heaven."

Before I continue, fear not! For countless reasons, this book will spend no time mimicking anything close to a scholarly text in theology. It won't have what it takes, because I certainly don't. And I wouldn't make the attempt even if I thought I could. To scoop my own goods, I best explained my hopes for readers in the book *Bent Hope,* which remains the same here: "What follows is extended to all for your consideration, deliberation and reflection: Those who believe there is no God, those who hate God, those who struggle with God, those who believe in another one, and those who believe in Him as Abba Father alike..."

But to couch the stories that follow, and gather them together purpose-fully, these are the basics of my understanding and belief. Beautiful, gloriously confusing and all things in-between is the full interpretation of the Kingdom of God. But what I feel certain of is that the gospel (or "Good News") of the Kingdom of God is the New Testament's underlining and central theme. And that while Jesus makes it clear "My kingdom is not of this world" (John 18:36), but an eternal continuum, it still includes being manifested "in" this world. Thus—on earth as it is in heaven. And if so, of all the teachings I have heard, read or sensed as absolute, none moves me more than knowing that the grace-dynamic of God causes the Kingdom to function.

Then, stepping way outside anything I have heard anyone speak or teach on, my gut simply tells me this: ultimately, the whole thing is about celebration.

In this life, we all celebrate most and best in the places—and with the people—where we feel we belong. I can imagine it no different in God's Kingdom. That this too is His will "on earth as it is in heaven."

So how do we go about fitting in? Truly belonging so that we can truly cel-ebrate? Any of us, all of us, trapped in our own freakish, misfitting, lost cause insecurities and frailties? My suggestion, while offsetting at first glance, is blunt.

Give up.

Each and every one of us should give up. Without question. If you make it to the end of the book assuming I am suggesting any one thing, let it be this: you and I should completely give up.

Before you slam this book shut, certain that I have supplied the most pathetic and despairing advice to ever reach published pages, allow me to explain. By no means am I implying that we should give up according to the expression as it's currently and commonly understood. We should look at what the union of the words should *really* mean by looking at what each one *does* mean.

Give: to present voluntarily and without expecting compensation; to place in someone's care; to grant; to provide; to produce.

Up: toward or in a more elevated position, or to be in a state of enthusiastic or confident readiness.

How on earth did it become anything but wonderful to *give up?* This mar-riage of words should've been destined as a phrase expounding God's calling for every human being on earth. To drive the point home, putting opposites into play (while firmly believing that the opposite of "give" here is not "take" but "keep"), the contrary would be to "keep down."

It's perplexing how it missed association with positive slang prose like "go for it," "hang in there" and "way to go." Coaches should be telling their teams to get out there and *"Give up!"* Directors should be telling aspiring actresses and actors that the only way to succeed is to *"Give up!"* Moms and dads should be teaching small children to be polite, play safe and *"Give up!"*

In all ways and in all things.

In few scenarios might this re-instalment of the informal be as poignant, both literally and figuratively, as with a homeless teenager I knew named Jeremy. I had mentioned to him that I would be in the downtown core late one autumn evening, after attending a friend's book launch. We arranged to meet at one of the corners he would frequent to panhandle and people watch. Somewhere around 11 p.m. on that cool October evening, I arrived on the scene with hot chocolate and pizza. But he was nowhere to be found.

In general, with most of my friends on the street, any prearranged plan was an uncertain proposition at best. Drug busts, dirty deeds, deep cover, thug fests, transient tendencies, gutter illness and assorted states of consciousness might impact even the best-laid plans. But Jeremy was a different sort. If he said it, he meant it. And he expected the same in return.

While I was surprised that he wasn't there, I was more worried than curious. He worked to keep his nose clean and head up. The only times he had not been where he said he would be were the times when he was in hospital or in custody. And I had only known either to happen when his solitary crime was being in the wrong place at the wrong time. Easy to do when the streets are home.

Jeremy was a bright boy with a courageous heart and a tragic story. But the street doesn't care about that. The street acts like a spider on a web, snaring prey that had expected to simply fly by, winding ugly cocoons for the street *status quo.* On the inside, each one is unique in the details, dreams of much more, feels stuck with few options, struggles to survive and does what they must, for better or worse. But to the busy passerby, they all look the same. North American Homelessness 101. Jeremy's lot.

I circled the sidewalk and peered down the streets. Though it was late, it was Friday night on the tourist track, the bar scene was buzzing, and it was a long while till winter, so there were people-a-plenty. Sightseers, late-shifters, partiers and players all passed by. But no Jeremy.

Then, from out of nowhere, my name. Or so I thought. Left, right, in front, behind. I spun twice.

Nothing. Mistaken, I'd guessed.

But it came again. Just a bit louder. Three rotations later, no Jeremy in sight. And no one I knew or who even cared I was there. I was all but ready to answer in a fit of unpreparedness, "Yes, Lord, here am I," when laughter rolled down.

"Up here! I'm up here!"

Sure enough, just above a small boulevard wedge, in a modest city-placed tree, a teenage boy playing Tom Sawyer. I walked beneath his roost inconspicuously, in an attempt not to compromise his cover, and looked up slowly. I will never understand how he accomplished it, but he had pulley-systemed an abandoned skid that he'd found behind a dumpy restaurant into the branches, concocting a makeshift tree fort, high enough to go unnoticed. Not along the secluded greenery near the river or in one of the abandoned warehouse yards near the lake, but along one of the most travelled sections of an inner-city main street in all of the nation. It was remarkable. Heading into my third decade of street work, this was, for me, yet another first.

Uncertain of what exactly he expected me to do, I held the pizza and cardboard cup tray above my head toward him—to take if he wanted, to show in the least. A *give up,* you might say.

"Comin' down," he chimed, his feet already hanging. A ten-foot hang drop, a quick tuck, and he stood looking pleased.

"Pizza! Great man. Thanks," he said with a wide grin and outstretched hands.

I handed the small flat box to him and asked, "What are you doing up there?"

His reply was succinct and profound. Ingenious and sad. Fascinating and heartbreaking. All the things Jeremy was. He opened the box lid, smelled the food with his eyes closed, and shut it. Then he looked me in the eyes, dropped his shoulders, dropped his smile and dropped his voice.

"Just tired of everyone looking down on me."

And there it is. The long and short of humanity. Heartbreak of the Creator. Illumination as to why a Messiah had to come. More packed in a single statement than a sea of poets and musicians could hope to contextualize in a collective body of works. All unassumingly surrendered in eight words by of one of society's nobodies. An outsider, looking in, wishing he belonged so he could celebrate.

When my book *Bent Hope* was released, I had no idea what to expect. I had hoped my publisher might be able to give me word on a regular basis that X number of people bothered to check it out. But I would never have guessed that people would write to me in such volume and with such emotion and depth, eager to tell their own stories and share in an unsolicited union with the beautiful and broken souls in the book's chapters.

Messages from around the world found me, affirming what I had always believed: none of us feel we belong when we are looked down on. And when we do, it's hard enough to survive, nevertheless try to celebrate.

And so this book is an ode to celebration, and those who seek and cherish it. Not celebration of the rose-coloured glasses kind, but of the when-you-least-expect-it kind. A tribute to those who reveal light and broker joy when the odds are clearly stacked against them. Quite often when they don't even know they're doing it. A bow to those who are at the very centre of God's Kingdom, unbeknownst to anyone but onlooking angels. And a tip of the hat to those who have found a way to celebrate in the moment, knowing that everything could change in a heartbeat. Just like dancing with dynamite.

I had some sense of taking this direction for a follow-up to *Bent Hope* within weeks of its release. But the real kicker came only three months later, after speaking at a national conference on the Canadian prairies. A woman I didn't know at the time came to me with her husband (now dear friends of mine) and with tears rolling down her cheeks said, "I don't know why, but I have to tell you this story."

They had moved their entire family from the west coast to another city, in another province, simply because they adored their daughter. Not because she was winning dance awards or was a prized athlete. Not because her scholastic ability opened doors to finer academic institutions. Simply because they adored her, the way God adores His own broken children. The middle child of three girls, Alexa suffers with the severe effects of the life-long brain disorder, autism. There was no sufficient support system available in the city where they lived to assist them in managing their daughter's extreme tantrums and outbursts in their household. And they longed to do anything and everything possible to keep her at home, rather than in a special facility. So they moved to a city with a few more in-home services. Courageous and costly in every way imaginable.

Autism is a spectrum disorder, varying in symptoms ranging in severity and impact from person to person. The parents and siblings of children with severe autism don't have the luxury of choosing when to be heroic or brave or tender or wise or composed. They are forced to surrender whatever portion of each of these virtues they can muster every single day, often fighting against believing that God owes them anything less than an IOU.

One day, Alexa had one of her most robust emotional and physical fits. To make things even more complicated, she had grown into a large girl for her young age of 11. Mom and dad were forced to restrain her and hold her on the ground while she flailed and fought, tortured by an inexplicable malfunction of the brain resulting in radical behaviours. One of the worst episodes of her young life during one of the last gasps of her parents' stay-at-home efforts.

Then from out of nowhere, something extraordinary happened. Between thrashes and screams, tears and sweat, with mom and dad both holding her to the ground with their body weight, she began to sing. Not just any song. Not a song she had even heard recently, or often. But one from a children's movie she had not seen in many years. From Disney's 1989 release *The Little Mermaid,* the song "Part of Your World." Lyrics that end with:

> When's it my turn?
> Wouldn't I love,
> Love to explore that shore up above
> Out of the sea
> Wish I could be
> Part of that world.

Where does Alexa belong?

How many people unacquainted with severe autism would think she belongs with them? In line with her mom at your grocery store? Waiting at your auto shop with her dad? Watching her sister at a little league game? How many who know better would truly believe or feel any different? What kind of trees, and just how many, would she have to climb to not be looked down on? And just when does her celebration begin? Certainly, the odds could not be stacked against her much more than they already are.

I have no answers. But I have witnessed, heard and been among those who do. Some were my friends. Some are my friends. Some were simply friendly encounters. Some were and are complete strangers. There is a pseudonym here and a non-specific there in a few cases to guard the confidence of some. There is also the courageous transparency of many who have allowed their great hearts to be exposed for this book—that somehow their souls would find yours. This is their book. These are their answers.

I'm not sure where this book will end up or who will hold it in their hands. It's an awkward thing to write for people who know you, and even stranger to write for strangers. The tenor of my publisher's slate of authors as I know it projects a much more conservative tone than do I. While I don't apologize for that, I am also wary of offending good-natured readers looking for gentle words and soft stories. The plain truth is this: I am as—or more—hopeful that this book will be on the bedside stand of someone waking up from a hangover during a university frosh week as I am that it's being read as Bible college curriculum. That it sits beside as many crack pipes as it does tea cups. That it's read behind prison bars as often as it's read from easy chairs. That it finds as many people hooked up to hospital tubes as it does people in trendy coffee nooks. I pray that as many—if not more—people who feel they don't know God's love read this as those who do. And in all of those hopes and prayers, I trust that God can make any words good when they're spoken in love.

Mere words, followed by more words on a page as you flip through them. It's easy to put words and more words on paper. But they are not offered to you as words, pages or a book. They are humbly presented as gentle reminders to seek out splendour and anticipate finding it. Each chapter is simply a testimonial that the most powerless people in all of society ironically carry the most powerful and eternal messages imaginable. People who have learned to *give up* rather than simply give up. I can only pray that my feeble words do them some justice. That my words celebrate them.

But my deeper prayer is that if you recognize that Alexa belongs in God's Kingdom as His beloved, and if you recognize that Jeremy belongs in God's Kingdom as His beloved, and if you recognize that the breathtaking and beautiful outsiders in this book are supernaturally sublime in their belonging—that surely you would recognize one more thing:

You belong there too.

"Doctor John Langdon Down, 1866. Do you know him? Do you? Ah, c'mon, do you or don't you?" Oscar interrogated me the moment I walked through the front door for the first time, before I could even begin to squeeze out any kind of a greeting.

"Oscar, at least let him get through the door and meet you," the on-site nurse reprimanded him as she nodded and smiled at me.

But Oscar was relentless.

"He invented idiots and imbeciles, that Doctor John Langdon Down did. Idiots and imbeciles, woo-hoo!" he cackled, and ran away down the hall, giggling.

"No he didn't! He classified them a long, long time ago! It meant something different way back then! We've had this discussion countless times, Oscar! Those are not nice words anymore!" the sweet nurse shouted out from the kitchen with a reluctant grin.

Then she turned to me and cocked her head. "Welcome. You must be Tim. That is..." She sighed and cleared her throat, "Um, Oscar."

In the distance, Oscar's muffled voice continued from behind his bedroom door. "Idiots and imbeciles, idiots and imbeciles, woo-hoo! That Doctor John Langdon Down was something else!"

Oscar was pear shaped and barely four feet tall at age 22. In all my years of working in group homes and what were then called "special needs facilities and camps," I never met another individual so aware, knowledgeable and hilarious about his own complex challenges and genetic makeup. He knew more about Down syndrome than any of the staff. I was in college at the time, studying syndromes, genetics and cognitive development as part of completing a developmental service worker diploma. I had many part-time jobs, placements and volunteer positions in residential and institutional settings throughout my college years. However, none of these experiences, or any formal schooling, tutored me the way Oscar unintentionally did while I was serving at his group home.

Nothing was out of bounds for Oscar. Especially around the topic of Down syndrome, which he studied endlessly and had his own take on. Mealtimes were served up with Oscar's generous series of single and out-of-context words and sentences, spoken with a full mouth, between bites.

"Action T-4. The Nazis would have murdered me."

Spoonful of corn.

"Genetic material on the 21st chromosome, that's the issue."

Forkful of beans.

"Nondisjunction. Nondisjunction."

Swig of milk.

But for me, Oscar was at his fascinating best when he used his knowledge for sly comedic effect.

He loved to put the flat back of his head against the wall and say, "Look at me, coming from out of nowhere." Or he'd playfully push me as though provoking fisticuffs and say, "You think I'm mentally retarded, don't you! Don't you! Well, put your dukes up! I'll show you who's retarded!" And one of his favourite things to do was to stick out his long, thick, pointed tongue as far as he could and say, "You don't even want to know the damage this can do."

I never sensed he really meant it in any sexual way—he was just very aware of the difference in his tongue from everyone else's. And he was proud of it. Still, it always got him a half-hearted scolding from staff and a very terse "You're gross" from the other residents. Particularly from Sheila, who not so secretly had a crush on him. As he did her.

But at his best, naughtiest, and everything in-between, one thing was clear: Oscar owned this home. His mood set the tone for everyone for the entire day. On days when he was grumpy, he possessed the power to bring grey clouds right into the room with him. He could design the day with a woeful grunt, or pattern the next 24 hours off a dramatic shrug and snort. And if you didn't share his disdain, he kept coming at you until you did.

But this was rare. At his usual best, he was a beacon. His quotes were "the" repeated and keeper ones. His laugh was infectious, his voice was dynamic, and his presence was electric. When he was on and in the room, everyone felt more alive.

At no time was this more evident than when any kind of celebration was at hand. Oscar was Brother Birthday, Captain Christmas and the tooth fairy's sidekick all rolled into one. No event was too small to turn into a party. During my time there, Oscar organized and resided over house parties for everything from a funeral and wake for a baby robin that fell from a backyard tree, to a graduation ceremony for one of the residents who learned to tie her shoes. And not just spur-of-the-moment parties. That was unthinkable. He wanted to create working committees, delegate responsibilities and make "coming event" posters. He was an all-or-nothing guy, who always chose "all."

It was during a dry celebration season on the calendar that Oscar hatched a new party scheme. Between April and May, there were no real holiday events or house birthdays to commemorate, so Oscar lobbied for a dance party. He pitched a Sadie Hawkins dance, a costume ball and a luau, all to no avail. Each one considered somewhat lofty for a household of seven. But he met the staff halfway with a more modest festivity in the form of an agreed-upon spring dance.

Anything to break out the "blue boogie dogs." That was what Oscar called his special blue high-top sneakers, which he saved solely for dance occasions.

A date was chosen and circled on the large kitchen calendar, and the one-week countdown began. And so did Oscar's very serious and thorough to-do lists. He organized a decorating committee, a music committee, a refreshments committee, an advertising committee, a greeters' committee, and on and on. There was even a wardrobe committee responsible for making sure that everyone came in spring attire. While most of the staff and residents had to sit on three or four committees, simply because there were as many committees as people, Oscar sat on and chaired them all, as the self-imposed and proclaimed event coordinator and master of ceremonies.

The end of day six came slowly. Oscar had been a taskmaster from beginning to end, and throughout the week there was never any allowance for conversation about anything that was not in one way or another related to the spring dance. As bedtime for the residents finally rolled around on that final day, I was putting away towels in the hallway linen closet, right across from Oscar's room. Those moments became some of the most profound in my lifetime. It was there that I could hear Oscar saying his bedtime prayers.

Oscar prayed for God to help him sleep, because he was so excited. Then he went on to explain to God that he was not as excited as on Christmas Eve, but more excited than the night before St. Patrick's Day—kind of somewhere in-between. He lost focus and began talking about how excited he gets on Christmas Eve, knowing Santa and his eight reindeer are on the way (adding, "nine if you count Rudolph, but he is not one of the originals, so you can't always count on it"), then caught himself and assured God that he was just as excited that it was the baby Jesus' birthday too.

He got his prayers on track with an "Okay, Heavenly Father, back to the dance....," and prayed for each committee one by one. He prayed that the Kool-Aid would not be too sweet, and still not too watered down. And that there would be enough of the red and orange Kool-Aid, because no one liked the green stuff. He prayed that people would really think through what to wear and not just show up in "any old thing."

My silent position was all but compromised with muffled laughter when he prayed that God would help him remember all his best dance moves, and that Sheila would like them.

But the best was saved for last. He closed by praying for each resident, one by one. Then each person on staff, one by one. Name by name. That each one of us would "have a fun time and forget our worries for a little while." And in that very moment, I could feel Oscar's heart beating in rhythm with God's own in a way I was sure mine never had. That Oscar could pray such a thing for me, while knowing only too well—and better than most—all of the obstacles and challenges in his life, completely overwhelmed me.

He said his amen, and then in a manner I could only imagine made the maker of the sun, moon and stars Himself chuckle, he added, "P.S. Heavenly Father, I think I offended Sheila today. If I did, I am sorry. If not, then never mind."

Brilliant.

Finally, the big day came. A bright, sunny Sunday. As beautiful as it was, the morning was nothing but agonizing for Oscar—which translated into agony for everyone—as the 2 p.m. start time took forever to arrive. But when it did, Oscar did not miss a beat, and did not disappoint. He left his clipboard behind and put on his finest party hat. He worked the room like an ambassador. Glad-handing and small-talking like an aristocrat who'd invited everyone who's anyone. He was jolly with big shy Paulie. He was buddy-buddy with sporty Clifford. He was gentle with mousey Alita. And he was charming and smooth with Sheila, of course.

And he danced! Oh, he danced! Not simply like people do when attending a dance party. Oscar danced the way songwriters describe dancing in heaven when they talk about being in the presence of God. His tiny eyes were shut tight, his little hands would wiggle in the air, and his head would bob to one side while his hips bounced to the other. He was extraordinary. And at the start of every song and several times throughout, he would open his eyes and take note of anyone not moving to the beat and shout at them, "Dance while you can! Dance while you can!"

Because we knew he would dance nonstop and put his complex body at risk, we had convinced him that there should be a "socializing break" between songs. He loved the idea, and thought it was so he could schmooze and make sure everyone was having a good time. And that he did. But when that music started up, he went into full groove.

With the sly advantage of chairing the music committee, Oscar had sorted out a different dance move for every song, calling them out by name as he performed them. The blue boogie dogs were more than alive and well. Somewhere between the hustle and the mashed potato, he had even calculated a moment to invite Sheila to slow dance with him. He was in his glory.

Three twenty-five p.m. came, and it was nearly time for the party to end. Oscar crawled onto the coffee table, a big wet mess. His hair was standing on end, one side of his shirt was untucked, and he had cookie crumbs and Kool-Aid stains on his face. But once he balanced himself on the small oak table, he was nothing shy of the emperor.

"I'd like to thank everyone for attending the first annual spring dance," he said with great distinction.

I looked at another staff member and smiled. No one had agreed on the "annual" part. He continued by thanking each committee, and then launched into his final announcement.

"As a special treat," he continued, "we will end with my presentation of the electric slide."

He pointed at Shelia, who he had prearranged would push play on the tape deck, on cue.

And it happened, just as planned. Click. And he bounced off the coffee table, boogying to the theme from *Saturday Night Fever*. And electric slide he did. Along with every other dance move he had seen, heard of, or could make up in the moment, all the while calling out to every wallflower and person not bobbing to the beat, "Dance while you can! Dance while you can!"

The party ended, noted by all in attendance as the best house party ever. And truly it was that, and more. Of all the parties I have ever attended in my lifetime, none has ever been more memorable or more vivid in my mind.

Oscar ate well that night. He laughed and played "remember when" all evening about the party as though it had happened years ago. He had a bath, had his snack and said his prayers, like every other night. Woke up to porridge, half a banana and orange juice in his favourite Batman cup, and prepared for his day program like every other weekday morning. He took his lunch out of the fridge, said his goodbyes and stood on the front stoop to wait for his bus. The little bus pulled up at 8:45 a.m. and Oscar was on his way. Just as he had done countless times before.

But Oscar never came back. He had a seizure while at his day program. This was not uncommon. But through a series of complexities, this particularly severe seizure had great ramifications to his congenital heart defects. It was later diagnosed that it was in no way linked to overexertion of any kind. These complications and threats had been looming his entire life. In fact, most of the scares around his past chest and heart pains came the very few times he was too *inactive.*

I only worked at that particular group home for another month or so. The first week after Oscar was gone, the grief was palpable. No one knew what to do or what to say. Or so I thought. We on staff tried to speak comfort and reassurance to the residents, but nothing we said hit the mark. For me, the world didn't look the same, and God seemed a thief. My attempts were authentic, but my heart was in betrayal. That was until big, bumbling Paulie stopped me midway through one of my lost causes, babbling sentences about it being okay to cry. He put his heavy arm around me and simply said, "We all hurt the same."

I had taken no cues from the renowned L'Arche communities around the world. I was dug deep in the "us and them" of staff and resident—titles created by humans that often surrender the most significant notions of humanity and godliness. Ones that can thwart the opportunity for authentic community when given too much power.

Paulie walked away. But not before I noticed a small, nuanced behaviour. He stepped very gently through the hallway, past the side door. I wondered why. It was very uncharacteristic. I watched him closely but could not put it all together until I looked past the furniture obstructing my view.

There it was. The answer. Not just how they were coping, but how they were healing.

Oscar's special blue high-top running shoes were left at the side door. They had not moved since the dance. And they weren't going to.

Without anyone speaking a word, Oscar's dearest friends had very purposefully left his special shoes untouched as a memorial to him. There was little or no access to gravesites and tombstone visits in their world. As staff, thick in policies and academic responses, our attempts to truly provide comfort were feeble at best. But they knew better anyway. There was more life and healing found in looking upon those worn sneakers, and pondering their purpose and owner, than any stone monument could have ever offered.

I will never forget the last day I worked at the home. I came from the basement without being noticed, only to find Sheila sitting cross-legged only inches in front of the shoes, weeping. Then laughing. Weeping. Then laughing. Experiencing grief as she should. And life as she must.

Oscar didn't just know what the key to life was. He didn't simply sense what God really wants from us. He lived and laughed and loved all in the centre of it, being this:

> Not only should we all dance while we can. Of course. For Oscar that would've been completely obvious. But that we find ways for others to do the same. Oscar was thrilled to dance and was on fire that everyone would have the same chance. But his greatest joy always came when everyone did.

Ironically, the influential and controversial nineteenth-century German philosopher Friedrich Wilhelm Nietzsche, who turned his back on his faith at a young age while studying theology, and who eventually ended up incapacitated by complete insanity, said it best: "I would believe only in a God that knows how to dance."

And so would I.

And so would Oscar.

And so I do.

We are all created in the image of God. Not some, but all.
True or false?

The biblical, Christianity-subscribed answer is yes. Certainly, the beliefs and practices of other monotheistic religions support this view, regardless of great variances in dogma. And, all theology aside, at least the sensibility of it is a sweet, social-justice friendly, politically correct sentiment.

Theologians, philosophers, mystics and maniacs from temples to cyberspace have unpacked the guts out of this notion. From the most revered scholars in history to the most prestigious thinkers and writers of the modern age, no stone has been left unturned in an effort to stitch together the genesis of Genesis with the realities of everyday life. But if so many people subscribe to this as truth, at best, or hopeful notion as second-best, then why do our actions so constantly repel it, or ignore it?

I had waded through an endless stream of dissertations and expositions on this truth flowing from the most eloquent sages in history, from the sublime to the transcendent. But none of them had anything on a terrified and bewildered 14-year-old, tapping on my screen door well after midnight.

My very first venture into what felt like the "otherworldliness" of what were then called "special needs" came when I was 16 years old. I was playing in a young rock band with my best buddy, Derek, whose father and family had founded a renowned camp for deaf children. Derek told me that he couldn't do band practices through the summer months because he would be up north serving at this camp. I was intrigued, and asked for the chance to tag along and get involved. What I had naïvely thought might be a bit of fun in the sun with a bunch of children who could not hear unfolded into a tableau for the design of my life, up to this very moment, and no doubt until the end of my days.

The Ontario Camp of the Deaf sits on one of the most beautiful parcels of land in all of Canada, sandwiched between two serene private lakes, hidden in the breathtaking garden of the great Muskokas. The camp was founded in 1960 by Bob and Mary-Jean Rumball. Bob Rumball was a professional football player and ordained reverend who immersed himself and his family in service to and among the deaf community, and went on to pave the way for reforms for deaf and developmentally challenged children and adults in education, employment, psychiatric care and the justice system. But I knew little of Bob Rumball's great and growing legacy as a 16-year-old. At the time, to me, he was just my best friend's dad. That too would soon change.

The six-week camp program was broken into three sessions of 14 days each. Two weeks of senior camp: preteens and teens. Two weeks of junior camp: children between the ages of four and 11. And two weeks of special camp: for campers of all ages, youth through adult, whom we called "deaf-plus," referencing that they were challenged with mild to severe developmental and physical challenges in addition to being deaf.

My first dose of reality, a signpost that this was not going to be a cakewalk, came only minutes after the first camp session had officially begun. I had gone up to the camp with Derek a few hours before the first bus full of campers was to arrive. I stumbled my way through a handful of greetings with some of the deaf and hard of hearing staff, all graciously either reading my lips or suffering through my painfully slow fingerspelling. I remember thinking–*Wow. That wasn't simple.* But I had no idea how un-simple my world was about to get.

The sound of the bus' grinding gears and a cloud of the gravel road's dust arrived at the top of the camp hill long before the bus itself. But when it finally did appear, the half-minute between camp entrance and dining hall was more than enough time for me to second-guess my being there. Hands, heads and entire torsos were squeezed through the second-hand school bus' windows. Shrieks and shrills of joy rang out from the 64-seater as adolescent campers celebrated the end of the long journey from the muggy metropolis to a bit of paradise. I will never forget being shocked by the sheer volume. In my ignorance, I had somehow imagined a gang of young deaf people being very quiet, rather than simply being as all young people are. Or better still, for good reason, even louder.

The bus pulled up only paces from the dining hall doors. Luggage and sleeping bags were matters for later–supper was served. Straight to the dining tables was the plan. The bus doors yawned open and young people literally poured out. Three and four at a time through the same 30-inch passageway, hooting and hollering. What came next was extraordinary, beautiful and spellbinding all at once. But most of all, for remarkably ill-equipped me, it was just plain petrifying. *Sign language.* Not sign language like I had anticipated by strumming through look-and-learn books and attending a few once-a-week beginner classes. This was the real deal. Deaf from birth, mile-a-minute deaf culture, talking hands sign language. The kids knew it, the staff knew it, the bus driver knew it, and if that weren't enough, even the camp dog had been taught to respond to signs. I have since travelled all over the world, visiting a myriad of countries that speak languages I don't understand, but never have I come close to feeling as dislocated as I did in those moments.

Eleven campers. Five down each side and one at the end. Five minutes in, and I was sitting at the head of a table residing over the suppertime well-being of 11 campers, predominantly around my age, and even some older, all of them proficient in two things. One—sign language. Two—sensing a heyday in store by scoring a camp counsellor who didn't have a clue. It was akin to a time I recall in elementary school when they couldn't find a supply for an absent school-teacher, so they sent in the janitor's part-time assistant, just to have an adult in the room. We made the most of our luck that day.

As supper was served, I knew my presence was the only conversation being had. Nearly a dozen campers, each one skilfully signing with one hand and manning a fork with the other, and never needing to slow down or take a pause when their mouths were full. Signing anything and everything, right in front of me, knowing I couldn't even guess at what they were really saying. Just that I knew it was about me. They would look at me, then one would sign something and the other would laugh. Back and forth in pairs and small groups, eyeing me, grinning, signing and giggling. An initiation well deserved, when you con-sider the number of times each one of them might have felt the same with the roles reversed on the subway, in the library or in the mall.

Ten minutes in and I had not been able to unload more than two "Hellos," one "It's hot" and one painfully long "My name is T–I–M." It was agony. Then finally, the camper at the end of the table waved his hands at me to get my attention. He was the last guy I wanted to be tested by, if for no other reason than he seemed more man than me. I was barely shaving, and he had a reason-ably good start on a teen moustache and bottom lip soul patch.

He tapped the index and middle fingers of his right hand back and forth over the same fingers on his left. I breathed a sigh of relief. This one I knew. Or thought I did.

"Chair," I mouthed back proudly, before even considering why he would sign that to me from out of nowhere. He laughed out loud and signed it again, while all ten of the other campers looked on.

"Yes, chaaaaair," I mouthed back at length like a complete fool. And everyone laughed.

He signed it one more time. So I stood and looked at my chair, and the table exploded with laughter.

I sat down and the camper stood. He pulled back his own chair and walked toward me, slowly. All but strutting, to draw it out. He got to my end of the table and leaned over slowly, right in front of me. Then, like a surgeon removing shrapnel from a vital organ, he plucked up the salt shaker that was six inches from my plate, held it front of my nose and said in a perfectly understandable and clear voice: "Salt."

Sure enough, the sign for salt is two wiggling tapping fingers over two wiggling tapping fingers, while the sign for chair (more specifically "seat") is those same fingers tapping in unison.

He sauntered back to his seat like the cat that caught the mouse, heroic to his buddies. And that same boy asked me for the salt at every single meal for the next two weeks, including at breakfasts, when there was no salt on the table. He also became one of my best on-site teachers and favourite campers, while never, ever, releasing me from his barbs and saucy manner.

I hung in through the summer. The senior campers eased up, the junior campers were too preoccupied, and the special campers were either more forgiving or just plain didn't care. Through it all, the staff team was patient beyond measure. In addition, Derek had my back, his sisters gently coached me, and his mom was the camp nurse and always had an encouraging word and counsel for me.

I went on to serve at the camp for 15 entire summers, moving from a rookie know-nothing counsellor to the staff director by age 21. The first five summers I attended on student grants, and the following ten via an annual secondment from my employer, Youth Unlimited (Toronto YFC). Those summers at the camp shaped and challenged me in ways I could never have imagined. They gave me a testimonial of radical mistakes and priceless celebrations too abundant to measure. I made friends for life and secured memories that are legendary. And if all that were not enough at age 18 I met a beautiful young blonde on the camp hill and five years later married her.

But of all the memories that remain vivid in my mind, of all the dramatic scenarios that snuck up and knocked the wind out of me, of all the moments of inspiration, spectacle and challenge, few—if any—resound in my soul like the night with no names.

Try as we did, we never fully knew exactly how many campers were coming at any given time. Last-minute changes in group home scenarios and residential settings always thwarted camp arrival schedules, meal planning, event programming and cabin lists. While this added great complexity in planning for any of the sessions, "special camp" had its own unique trials and complications that made it almost impossible to prepare for. Among them were communications with government-run institutions for developmentally disabled people.

In 1876, Ontario's first institution, called the Ontario Asylum for Idiots, paved the way for several provincial institutions to follow, with a cumulative result of housing thousands of "feeble minded" residents. By the time I was serving at the camp, just over a century later, a long overdue change in philosophy had just begun to gain mainstream acceptance. Quality of life, community living and inclusion were controversial expressions of this new philosophy. Somewhere between pie-in-the-sky liberation and people warehousing, thoughtful minds began to tackle the challenges of effectively bestowing the rights of people with developmental disabilities into communities. A shift that was not simple then, and that remains contentious to this day. And a decade into my tenure at the camp, none of this changed the fact that residents from old school institutions were going to be dropped off on a Saturday afternoon into our charge.

For the most part, years of a history with the camp would dictate a master list of return campers. But inevitably there would be unexpected guests with conditions we were not equipped to facilitate. With the exception of a handful of students funded by federal grants, our camp was staffed by volunteers. Most of them university and high school students. When I started as a teenager, most of the staff were deaf, but in the ten years following, the configuration included many more hearing teenagers and young adults, eager to learn sign language and deaf culture by being immersed in it. Many as naïve as I was when I started.

One sunny late Saturday afternoon, the staff assembled on the volleyball court, as had become the norm, ready in team T-shirts to greet the next throng of campers. The junior campers of a two-week-long stint had left that same morning, and there had been just enough time for staff to do their laundry, take a swim, and maybe rush into town to buy a few personal supplies before a 45-minute staff meeting with the camp nurse to go over the profiles of the campers we believed were on their way. From medication alerts to behaviour analysis, the information mounted in addition to the stories of special camps past that had been told and retold through the day.

The camp bus and several conversion vans all arrived at the same time, filled with people of all shapes and sizes. Many of them shapes and sizes our young staff had never seen before. But as the guests arrived—some stumbling, some hobbling, some bounding—new staff were eased into the situation by simply assisting senior staff in helping with luggage and showing small gestures of welcome. Then began the grand parade of what would've been viewed as freaks and mutants only mere decades earlier. As always, as beautiful as it was interesting. Most of them, we of many years knew. Some new, whom we were aware of. And two or three surprises that we had come to anticipate, all relatively high functioning.

But just as the mass huddled around the bus, something unanticipated happened. An entire group of new faces and body forms appeared. A small group we didn't know and were not anticipating from a large institution. And not anywhere near what we had come to expect in receiving surprise guests. Physical and developmental challenges far beyond what our young staff and facilities were equipped for. The jaws dropped on even the most experienced among us.

But first things first, and a sense that we as leadership had it all under control prevailed. For the time being. With a calm resolve, counsellors and assistants were asked to shepherd folks and lug gear. While teams escorted the would-be campers to their accommodations, the leadership team gathered to discuss this unforeseen development. But all we came up with was the affirmation of our initial gut instincts: *Yikes!*

We had turned around camp guests before, returning them to their living venues and surrogate homes for their own well-being, if nothing else. But that usually came only after a couple of days of all-hands-on-deck effort to do everything we could to not have to. This was different. Our limitations were evident only minutes in as anticipated one-on-one situations became two-on-one and three-on-one musts. We weren't just shy on expertise—we just plain couldn't maintain the math required.

The front desks of institutions were difficult to get past by phone at the best of times, never mind at 5 p.m. on a summer Saturday when they were impossible to even get to. After several attempts, we knew we had to do our best through the night with what we had and try to call in a request for high-needs reprieve in the morning.

And so everyone was on people duty. Kitchen helpers, maintenance staff, anyone with an ounce of discretion was called into action as extra hands. And finally, night fell. Our young staff was exhausted, but very affirmed and relieved that the night was to be an exception to the full camp session. Tomorrow would be a new day, with some sensible resolve for everyone involved.

And so it seemed. Until just before midnight.

Bang! Bang!

Three young female staff members pounded on my door as though they'd seen a ghost. I rushed off with two and sent the other for Derek. He arrived as I was being debriefed. The front deck of the large pine dorm was buzzing with staff and a few campers who had woken in the kerfuffle. Still, the lights in the dorm remained off, weighing in on one evident advantage of being deaf: sleeping through noise.

With waving arms and giant gasps we were apprised of the situation. But even youthful dramatics did not prepare us for what was in store.

We entered the building with flashlights, stepping over duffle bags and suitcases as we wound our way past a series of bunk beds. The room was eerie with the sounds of clogged nasal passages and breathing defects, as lungs worked extra hard to bring oxygen to various sleepers.

Two beams of light bounced from side to side as we got closer to our destination, instantly uniting as we shone our flashlights toward the hissing sound in the corner.

The young staff had not been dramatic out of turn. In fact, their words and enthusiasm had not done the immediate image justice. Standing on the top bunk, rocking back and forth, less than four feet tall, weighing less than 60 lbs at best, and covered in her own feces, stood a girl whose name I didn't know. She had come from one of the institutions that sent the surprise guests and had been earmarked almost immediately as one of our turnaround cases. Her soiled hands were like three-pronged claws with webbing between the spikes, held at eye level as though protecting herself. Feces matted her hair, was smeared across her face and covered the walls behind her. She was both terrifying and terrified. This, the furthest image conceivable from that of happy summer campers playing in the sun. Or, I should think, of the image of God.

We stood in awe, lost for words or actions. Shining the light away at intervals to gain our own composure, and remorseful of adding to the indignity. We quickly discussed turning on the cabin lights so she would be less afraid of us, and would not be stuck peering into two shaky beams of light. But the room worked against us. We knew only too well who was sleeping in the surrounding bunks and the bedlam that would ensue if they woke to this spectacle.

After quick deliberation, we agreed on what had to be done. One—try to tell her what we were about to do. Two—do it. Derek and I had worked as a team in no-win situations before, but none seemed so extremely impossible as this. No one had signed up for this. Especially her.

I shone the light on Derek so that he could try and sign to her, but there was no change. The hissing and rocking continued as she began to wipe the feces from her body and throw it at us. We had no idea if she even knew remedial signs, let alone understood any part of what had occurred that brought her to this strange and frightful time and place.

So finally, armed with nothing more than old grey army blankets, we approached her. Each of us stood on separate sides of the bottom bunk and reached up to secure her. She flailed and kicked as we did all we could to gently remove her without waking the others.

The stench was unbearable and the awkwardness unimaginable—a memory that kept me sleepless for several days to come. But once in our arms, she quit fighting. Her messy little body loosened, almost giving way to signs that she was happy for whatever was coming next. Then, while holding her as firmly and gently as we could, we removed her in a way that felt regrettably and unavoidably like removing a rolled carpet. The best we could do was treat her as a priceless one.

Only minutes later, she was in the capable hands of the camp nurse in the well-lit infirmary, aided by senior female staff members and a bevy of others on call. Too exhausted to struggle, and with some notion of comfort, she was prayerfully bathed and monitored through the night, and sent back to who-knows-what in the morning. Leaving queries in her wake for even the most devout in faith.

Begging the question—Where does she fit into God's Kingdom? What part of God's image is she?

Born in a different century, she would've been burned alive, fed to wild animals or beheaded, seen as no less than the vilest outcome of tyrannical witchcraft and demonic invasion. Born in another decade in the century of her actual birth, she would have received electroshock therapy all of her days, only to be of real value in post-mortem dissection. As it was, the sanctity of her life was disparaged to an existence of simply being anywhere that could stomach her. We had but 18 hours with her. What humanity was mugged from a lifetime to that point, and in the seasons of life to follow. Did a doctor "regret to inform" a horrified mother upon the birth of a baby with claws and a hydrocephalic lobe? Was she taken away immediately to a place that "handles these kinds of tragedies"? How many years did she know nothing more than scheduled diaper changes and group hose-downs at 7 a.m., noon, 5 p.m. and bedtime, regardless of when bowel movements and voiding came? None of these would be unique to one like her. And squealing in the dark, covered in her own waste, ready to lurch like a rabid bat—who would dare call her "fearfully and wonderfully made" (Psalm 139:14, NIV)?

I think it's too easy to qualify the matter by stating that every person who is aware, regardless of mental faculties, reflects God's image. I believe that the faith philosophy of soul, body and spirit representing all humans, in all conditions, as evident likeness of the trinity is an unsatisfying truth. Not because this truth is lacking, or because God is lacking, but because I am lacking. I want more.

This, for me, is where the power of words ends. This is where I require evidence for my heart, and not a smattering more of convincing for my intellect. No less than when I compare proud and loud self-proclaimed evangelists, hollering God-talk with wagging fingers, against the quiet actions of a humble servant.

Upon returning to the girls' dorm, the buzz in the place was electric. Every wide-eyed soul had a story to tell. Each one, the same tale, told from her own perspective. Each one self-spun into the centre of the drama, adrenalized by a vacating fear.

"I couldn't believe it." "I knew something would happen." "I can't sleep. I'm going to have nightmares." "I'm still scared." "I want to go home."

They consoled one another into the night. And rightfully so. All of it much more than anyone had bargained for.

And I was no different. My own telling of it was ripe with "my" racing heart, "my" best attempts, and what "my" eyes saw. I returned to my cabin, situated directly across from the girls' dorm, and pondered the night while listening to voices in the distance reliving every detail.

Eventually, the murmuring faded and the long day caught up with everyone. But just moments after I turned out my cabin lights, it came. Evidence. Three words from another girl whose name I didn't know, who saw past her own sense of dilemma, revealing the only true way to see the image of God in one another. Three words contextualizing the case while pointing to the clear instruct of Proverbs 4:23—"Above all else, guard your heart, for it is the wellspring of life" (NIV).

Fourteen years old. Pretty and healthy. Arrived that very day. Quiet, shy, new to everything and everyone. Came to help babysit the young children of a few adult staff—a supposedly simple and soft entry point into camp involvement. Caught in the melee of an introductory night from hell.

She tapped quietly on my door. I turned on the front step light and peered through the screen.

In barely a whisper, she asked, "Is she okay?"

The wellspring of life! A young heart guarded from fear, ego, narcissism, critique, scrutiny and self-involvement. A young heart that could inexplicably associate with the brokenness and suffering of a life that could not be any more different from her own. A young heart that knew that "binding up the broken-hearted" must surely include those tortured in ways we cannot even comprehend. Discovering the image of God by caring about the extreme least of "the least of these."

She was the only one who asked.

The issue is never that the unsightly, incomprehensible, misshapen, misinterpreted and inexplicable are any more or less created in the image of God than anyone else. The real issue is the masses on the other side of the ledger who miss it.

The exquisite Jean Vanier wrote: "We tend to reduce being human to acquiring knowledge, power and social status. We have disregarded the heart, seeing it as a symbol of weakness, the centre of sentimentality and emotion, instead of as a powerhouse of love that can re-orient us from our self-centredness, revealing to us and to others the basic beauty of humanity, empowering us to grow."

"Yes. She's okay," I smiled, not even having a clue what "okay" would or should mean for her.

She simply nodded, turned and walked away. I forgot to ask her name.

The irony was staggering, if not just plain sad. There I stood in a Romanian grocery store, midway through one of the most profound weeks of my life, feeling both guilty and gleeful about the two-litre bottle of Coca-Cola in my hands. This was the night before we were heading to the poorest orphanage on our itinerary. The night with secrets for a soda pop Santa.

The "real" jolly old elf I once believed in, as most kids my age in Canada did, had his image surface on billboards and supermarket flyers every December, merrily posing with a bottle—*The Real Thing*—appearing perfectly magical in every way. The stark contrast to me in the moment was outrageous. Dishevelled and tired, still in half my unstuffed red velvet garb with undone suspenders hanging at my knees, sans the white fluffy beard and floppy red hat, sadly replaced by six days of stubble and an old baseball cap, longing for a sugary soda fix after a day of visiting children who literally had nothing.

But still, there I was indeed, as though transported into one of the surreal dreams that make you shake your head in the morning and say, "What was that all about?" Standing in an aisle of a grocery store filled with what would be considered food staples back home, but known as luxury items to a greater portion of this population, among slow-moving shoppers picking and choosing very thoughtfully and cautiously while suspiciously watching me as they passed by. In a country as foreign to me as foreign could be. And ready. Ah, so ready. Ready to reward myself, regardless of the irony or shame in it all.

I first heard about something called the "Romania Project" (now called "Impact Romania") early in the new millennium, one humid summer afternoon while visiting friends in Ontario's glorious Muskoka region. Just about as far away, in almost every way, as you can get from an orphanage in Romania.

Muskoka Woods has been best known in the mainstream as an esteemed Canadian sports camp since its inception in 1979. But its 30-plus-year history has always been that it is, in fact, so much more. Driven by leadership with an incredible capacity for not just thinking outside the box, but deciding there should be no box, and moving forward as such. And so, leaving assumptions behind, it is there that a unique vision spun into a passion, and a passion into a reality, creating a character-building bridge of opportunity for Canadians to give of themselves on behalf of Romanian orphans.

International Teams Canada assisted the effort with their support and expertise, and ultimately went on to champion the vision, under the leadership of Bob Fukumoto in 2005. Committed to building relationships with the Romanian orphan community, while mentoring young adult orphans as they build and maintain encouraging relationships with children still in orphanages, the Romania Project has proven itself to be life changing for countless people in Romania, Canada and around the world.

In general, I have always found it difficult to be near something that sounds so good and not try to wiggle my way in, see it for myself, or catch some of the energy in some small manner. Compounding my interest were two things. One—a growing desire to understand better, feel more intrinsically, and speak more knowledgeably about global social-justice issues. And two—unfinished business in my own heart from when it first broke over the issue of orphans while visiting Russia when I was a much younger man.

Still, no matter how sweetly someone can speak their heart over such things, or put it on paper, there is always something unequivocally self-serving in it all. While I am hesitant to say it is surely so for *everyone* who gets on board with a short-term missions project, my sense is that this is the quiet truth for most, and I know it is the absolute truth for me. Further, I truly believe that when we admit as much right from the get-go, we simply spare ourselves some small portion of the inevitable guilt and glory that runs rampant in returning-home testimonies wrought with self-awareness and navel-gazing. (Especially the ones we write about in books—sigh.)

So I signed on the dotted line, attended a couple of team prep meetings, wrote some soft support letters, chatted it up where chatting would help, and in a matter of weeks I was on my way to a city I hadn't even known existed three months earlier—Cluj. By the time we landed at our stopover in Vienna, I was able to count to ten and say 12 short and simple phrases in Romanian, which included "I'm from Canada" (which I was counting on as a likely excuse for a number of things) and "I'm sorry" (which I guessed might be more than appropriate on a number of occasions).

The tender hearts of the small team I was travelling with were both touching and evident from square one. Likewise, our leader, Bob, loved to get his people digging deep into their souls and sharing out loud what they'd found. It was abundantly clear that there would be no way to fly under the radar on this one. Joyfully and painfully, it was going to get messy.

Still, I guessed, I hoped, I prayed, my ace in the hole for a bit of emotional reprieve would be the role I had bargained my way into. A costumed role where I could simply act out a bit of make-believe when things were peaking in intensity. It felt like a great plan. One that would be uncontested and relatively simple to execute, I suspected, as no one in the short history of this expedition had filled these boots. Among all the previous Christmas teams that had ventured out, none had included a Santa Claus. But I came with the minimal requirements for the gig. I had the red suit, some experience in the red suit, and an airline ticket to Romania. Three check marks, one done deal. Clean and simple, I felt, rest assured. I have been endlessly wrong over an endless number of things in my life, but few times had I been this wrong. And in the end, never as thankfully so.

The history of Santa Claus is all over the map. In every way imaginable. It took him a long and complex journey, criss-crossing the globe and bouncing off centuries of myths and legends, to land his status and favour as the familiar, uncomplicated, jolly North American Santa depicted and immortalized in 1931 through a series of illustrated and still popular Coca-Cola ads. The one I would semi-successfully pretend to be at home, and now abroad.

As a bit of murky history tells it, the origin of the Christian-era Claus was Bishop Nicholas of Smyrna (Izmir), living in what is now known as Turkey, during the fourth century AD. Wealthy and generous, he would toss gifts and treats through the windows of poor children's homes. Variations on his story range widely, but what is known as apparent truth is that the Orthodox Church later esteemed a St. Nicholas by building what became Russia's oldest church in his honour, while the Roman Catholic Church dubbed a St. Nicholas as the patron saint of children and seafarers.

Whoever he was, or would become, in the minds of children of all ages around the world, from generation to generation, one thing was for sure: everyone wanted a piece of the action.

And so, many lifetimes before the information highway would allow for immediate identity theft, people still did what people do. Name it and claim it. In Protestant areas of Germany, St. Nicholas became known as *der Weinachtsmann.* England knows him as Father Christmas. In Sweden he is *Jultomten.* Then there's Spain's *Papa Noël,* Italy's *Babbo Natale,* Japan's *Hoteisho,* China's *Dun Che Lao Ren,* and India's *Ganesha.* And on and on it goes.

The American version of Saint Nick was inspired by Dutch settlers who landed in New York in the seventeenth century, based on the legend of Sinterklaas, and was eventually tweaked to American contentment by Clement Clarke Moore's 1823 poem *A Visit from St. Nicholas,* more commonly known as *'Twas The Night Before Christmas.*

But among the oddest and most convoluted series of Santa fables are those borne of Romanian lore. Brushing by yuletide nods to everything from werewolves to solar gods, the positioning of three Santa brothers is among the most prominent of tales within the ancient Romanian pantheon—Santa Nicholas, Santa Eve and Santa Claus.

While none of these Santas are anywhere near the cheerful cartoon version that the global mainstream is now happy to hang its hat on, Santa Nicholas at least leans toward a real character within the Christian writing of the saints. But past being a defender of the Christian faith and known for expressing his great generosity with gift-giving to children, further comparisons are bizarre at best. His MO also includes punishing disobedient children with a "proverbial rod" and appearing on a white horse at the first sign of snow to protect the sun so people won't be deprived of warmth and light.

However, the tall tale of his brothers, Santa Eve and Santa Claus, is even darker and stranger. As proprietors of large houses and stables, their mishmash of a story actually has them inside the nativity story. That messy hubbub includes one of them cutting the hands off his wife for secretly helping deliver Mary's baby, and runs the gamut of peculiar storylines all the way to a Santa death as a consequence for an absence of decency.

When I first casually suggested that while in Romania perhaps I could sport my getup and mimic the simple Claus I imagined, I had no clue that there was a massive, sticky spider's web of a history binding Santa's thorny DNA to this long-suffering nation. I had not meant to be naïve or presumptuous, but clearly I had been both.

Christmas is popularly known as *Mos Craciun* in Romania. By the time the twentieth century had arrived, much of the festivity and lore had simplified to include happy, if not modest, traditions and celebration. While much of that was abandoned in 1947 when Romania surrendered to the USSR during World War II, making it a communist republic, Christmas celebrations were observed once again in 1989 when the country regained its independence. By that time, technology was fast making the world a much smaller place, and capitalist societies were able to reach deep into the psyches of distant worlds—and especially into the hearts and imaginations of young people. Thus, by the time I popped up with a "Ho Ho Ho!" in a territory so ancient that it claims to have human fossils as old as 40,000 years, there was less commonly-known history to trample on, and greater liberty to exploit North Americana at will. And so, not knowing what else to do, as unobtrusively as possible, I did.

Our team of nine Canadians and one American, joined by a young but inspiring Romanian volunteer team, ventured out prayerfully, hoping and planning on bringing a bit of Christmas to orphans across the country. From Cluj, the third largest metropolis in the country, to Figa, a rural region that time, technology and prosperity have clearly turned their backs on, we travelled with joy and sorrow as our truest companions. Each child we met unintentionally carried the weight of the entire orphan population on his or her little shoulders, begging with wishful smiles and undiscerning long hugs to be sprung free into the magic world that we strangers must have come from.

Romania's orphanage system warehouses nearly 50,000 children in 940 orphanages, and another 10,000 children in private orphanages. A further 30,000 children reside in foster care. A great many of them have living parents who have abandoned them. The end result of Nicolae Ceausescu's tyrannical dictatorship and diabolical social engineering plot was that it ultimately resulted in mass poverty that engulfed the country and paved the way for the unimaginable travesty of state-run orphanages as an easy solution for broken families and desertion.

All of it was—and is—no less than completely shocking. In fact, so overwhelming that, more often than not, it felt impossible to comprehend, even while seeing it all first-hand. This too among the most common of Western-world missions trip commentaries upon homecoming.

It wasn't until day four of our priceless and exhausting journey that the staggering reality finally split me wide open. But it wasn't the common denominators exposed in countless global media features or vital world mission communications on this human tragedy that pierced my soul. Deplorable conditions, emaciated infants and toddlers, psychological damage and developmental delay run amuck, to name but a few.

Ultimately, it was the whisper of a little boy in the poorest of the poor orphanages we visited that tore me apart. A boy in Iliua.

At the Iliua orphanage, our gathering place was to be the dining room. What was different about this, in comparison to the other venues, was that this was its own small building at the hub of the complex, requiring an outdoor walk to reach it from any of the other quarters. The room was dank and dark, furnished by little more than tiny wooden chairs and wobbly little tables.

Nearly a hundred children live in the Iliua orphanage. Most of them very young. One of the many things that caught me off guard in some of the more rural orphanages was that the children wore their hats, coats and boots both indoors and outdoors, all day long, due to the harsh climate combined with the absence of indoor heating.

The basic routine for our team at each venue, in a nutshell, went like this. The team would arrive as early as permitted at any given orphanage. Bob and one of the local Romanian volunteers would often seek out the main adminis-trator and tend to the important business of formal greetings, relationship maintenance and expectations of the day. Upon his return, we were usually per-mitted to do a select number of things to create a day unlike all other days for the children. Set up craft supplies, prepare food and treats, arrange the gifts and supplies that donors had provided, decorate a common space where we would eventually meet the children, and discuss the plan of action for that par-ticular group according to the rules and allowances of the orphanage staff. At each location there was a series of specific guidelines and protocols we needed to agree to prior to proceeding. Some made sense; some didn't. Some we agreed to respectfully, some reluctantly. Some made me sad; many made me angry. But at the end of the day, we did what we were told, knowing that our visits were a luxury that could easily be denied if we were suspected of looking down our noses at the administration. Evidence—as if any were ever needed—that pride and politics know no bounds.

Before we had even seen a single child at Ili ua, this event had already struck me as a standout. While we prepared, the late afternoon sky grew sev-eral shades of green just before it turned black, and a heavy fog rolled in. Eerily reminiscent of stereotypical movie images of nearby Transylvania. The whole vibe felt charged with the challenge of creating Christmas when not only was the ludicrous social reality working against it, even the haunting climate was taking its best shot.

My appearance as Santa was always scripted as the program capper. I would just be me during the first half of the visits, sneak away an hour into it to get all Claused up, and reappear via Bob's grand introduction as "Mos Craciun." Generally, I liked that routine. But this time around was different. I wanted to stay being me. I just plain hated to miss any of the time with the kids there.

All of the children we'd met up till then were remarkably affectionate. But these ones were like no other children I'd met in my entire life. As they filed in by age groups, they lit up and raced toward us, embracing our team members in the most fascinating and heartbreaking manner imaginable. Within sec-onds, I found myself sitting on a tiny children's chair with two wee ones on each knee and one wrapped around my neck from behind. No cost for trust or proof of honour required. Just a relentless hunger for warmth and assurance and gentle humanity. And the grand wish for instant and unconditional love.

Just as fascinating, if not more, was what they wanted. *Nothing!* They recognized instantly that I could not understand their language and acted as though they suspected as much before they arrived, and didn't want to burden me with the tax of trying. So they just sat and snuggled and hugged as though I were their very own adoring daddy. The one they never knew. The one they dreamed of.

My mind spun, bumping into countless questions, concerns and emotions, with no singular train of thought—*How is this possible? Bob can't overscreen his volunteer teams? Jesus loves the little children, all the children of the world!*

Finally, I came to and scanned the room. Each team member was wrapped up in the same glorious dilemma. We all tried to move around the room at intervals, making sure each child had some special time up close with a visiting grown-up.

Soon enough, I got the nod from Bob. Time to prime Mos Craciun. I snuck out the side door and slid into the old team van to ready myself. It was dark and cold and awkward, but the location of the independent building, now filled with children, did not lend itself to any other perceivable options without creating a fuss. Ultimately, the facility administrator happened to pass by, noticed me struggling, and waved me toward his nearby office with a smile.

Dressed and set, I sat in that little office and waited for my cue from across the pathway. These were spectacular moments alone for me. Ones I will hold on to for a lifetime. Moments that have occurred too few times in my life. I was taught to pray and to believe in prayer at a very early age. And so I did. But prayer can stale into an "I should" or "I better" or "I can" or, worst of all, "it's just a habit" proposition, like anything else, when you forget your true position and purpose in the scheme of things. Especially public prayer.

But this time, I had it right. Listening to the sweet voices and laughter of profoundly poor children floating across the muddy corridor, I pleaded with the Almighty to truly be "father to the fatherless" and tearfully thanked Him that He allowed this night. One of far too few "I humbly come before you" prayers in my life.

When I entered the dimly lit mess hall, the room erupted. The bright red suit and snow white beard were electric against the drab colours of the walls and the winter garments worn by the children. The orphanage staff and our team worked hard to corral the children, but the most spirited ones continually found ways to squirm free beyond their reach to mob and smother me.

Where the adult population (especially those in their senior years) may have been skeptical of a one dimensional good-deed Santa showing up, in light of Romanian legend, these children were neither educated nor concerned with anything more than the simplistic soda pop version. I am so very in favour of young ones knowing and respecting the histories, journeys, tales and legends of their own cultures and peoples—but I could not have been happier than to think this one was lost on the children we met.

Eventually, the orphanage staff reined in the chaos, all were seated, and each child waited in anticipation for 30 seconds of one-on-one with Mos Craciun. One at a time, moving through the order by age, each child came forward to receive a special bag of goodies, a pair of new boots and a photo with Santa.

The execution of it all was a tribute to the insights of the teams that had gone before us, the life experiences of our Romanian volunteer team, having grown up in and around the orphanages, and the generosity of those back home. Part of our team's daily routine was to painstakingly prepare individual age-appropriate gift bags from supplies that had been shipped from Canada for this purpose. Each child at each orphanage we visited then received a package that included everything from colouring books to underwear and small toys to socks. But the deprivation of this particular locale drove some extra incentive, resulting in a new pair of boots for each child.

Even the photos were done righter than right, pre-arranged that we had the capacity to give the children their pictures with Santa right then and there. Nailing me with another shocker. Many of the children had never seen a picture of themselves before.

To watch the team in action was a gift to me all by itself. Tenderly, cheerfully and often tearfully, they would bring the children forward, one at a time, to receive their gifts and see Santa up close. Never once treated as a generic group of "poor orphans," but rather priceless little souls, detailed with individual dreams, hurts and fears, despite the commonality of their dilemma.

Some of the children ran to me full tilt, jumped on my lap and beamed from ear to ear. Some of the children tip-toed slowly and hesitantly, ecstatic from afar but nervous up close. Some of the youngest ones (as young as three years old) needed motherly hand-holding from a team member for extra assurance. And a number of them needed extra help to live out the unfamiliar moments of enjoying treats because their little bodies and minds faced physical and developmental challenges that set them apart.

But one by one they came, while I sat in place and waited, all the while stunned that God would have my journey in life come this way. All of it a battle for my wits and a stifling squeeze on my heart. I knew my role was to sell jolly and provide whimsy. But as I watched these astounding children approach me, one at a time, as I sat them on my knee, as I held them and they held me, all I wanted to do was bawl.

But that's not Santa's job. At least not the soda pop edition. The number one job is to "do" happy. And as absurd as all of it was—nine days' escape from my overly blessed, overly comfortable, overly accommodated life—I was sure of one thing: the sorry minimum I could offer these children then and there was a few seconds of relative "happy." And if that was too haughty, perhaps at least a tiny bit of escape from "sad." But any and all of it just plain impossible if Santa becomes a puddle.

Of course, there was a 20-second buffer between children as one would leave my side and another was called forward. It was during one of these gaps, about 15 minutes into this parade of eager participants, that I noticed a special boy. "Special" in that he was behaving differently from anyone else in the room. He looked to be about seven or eight years old. Just around the age where children look extra close for Santa imposters—wondering if the whole thing was on the up and up. He sat at a little table with some of his peers, who were all waiting until we reached their age group before they would be called forward. While his buddies talked and giggled, pointed and fussed all around him, he sat very still, leaning across the table with his chin in his hands.

Once I had realized that his gaze was relentlessly fixed on me, I began to acknowledge it during the seconds I had between kids. The first time, I simply winked at him. His head popped up and his eyes grew wide, unsure that it was meant for him. So I did it again, and smiled. His jaw dropped with delight. For the next 20 minutes, he and I exchanged nods, waves, winks and funny faces at calculated intervals.

Finally, we were nearing his table, and soon enough he would be at Santa's side. But as he recognized that, the gestures ended. I blinked, but no blink back. I wrinkled my nose, but nothing in return. I pulled my granny spectacles down and pulled my fake white bangs to the side to be sure what I was seeing was real. It was. Tears were rolling down his cheeks. Beyond looking heartbreakingly sad, he appeared to be stewing over something. Seriously concentrating harder than any little boy should ever have to, or want to.

At last his turn came. I was actually nervous. At the same time, I was very eager to have him come forward. We already had some kind of unspoken and peculiar connection that only he and I were aware of, and I did not want to disappoint him by not being who or what he wanted me to be. I thought he might inspect my fake beard and wig and notice something not quite right. Too few wrinkles on my face or a soft belly too pillow-like.

But by the time he arrived at my side, he had sorted out what he needed to do. Not wasting precious time on guesswork; he knew he had one minute tops if he played it right. So he hedged his bets that I just might be the real deal, plopped himself down on my knee, wrapped both arms around my shoulders, leaned into my ear and began whispering. Fast and furious, like there was no tomorrow.

Startled by it all, I was lost on what to do.

While many a person of outspoken spiritual faith (Christian and otherwise) scoffs at the commercialism wrapped up in Santa's modern identity, it's the magic side of Santa and the adoration of someone almost godly-good that fire up many of the hardliners. Some would go as far as calling it harmful and idolatry. In general, it's a wonky conversation as far as I'm concerned. One I spend little time processing or debating. Especially since the rate of growing out of believing in him is 100 per cent. I have simply chosen to celebrate the values he represents and the fun his soda pop fable allows.

But this wonderful boy threw me for a loop. He believed for different reasons. It wasn't just about fun and games and make-believe. His fluid whispers were almost prayerful. It was as though he had saved up everything in his soul, banking on an opportunity to spend it in the right place. When someone like no other would finally come, as improbable as it would seem. Someone like Santa Claus coming to his lowly orphanage? No—someone *exactly* like Santa Claus.

To this day, even as I write these words, I am unresolved that I did the right thing, but know that I would do it again all the same.

I nodded, and hm-mm-ed as though I understood every single word. And he pressed on, believing I did.

When any of the other children spoke to me, one of the Romanian volunteers was always near to interpret. So there was never any fear of making painful promises with smiles and nods. But I couldn't chance breaking his focus and stride, and ultimately breaking his heart.

So I played it. I played it hard. Not because I thought he was asking for something I couldn't provide or make happen. If I'd really sensed that, I may have deliberated differently. Hard to know for certain. But because I truly believed that all he really wanted was to tell me his secrets. To tell someone who would listen and not judge. Someone outside of the shame, pain and despair. Someone who maybe knew other little orphans who had whispered the same kinds of things. I had no intention of playing God with this little boy and his secrets. But I chose to respond the way I desperately hope God responds when He hears mine.

One of the gatekeepers to my well-being is a wonderful woman named Sharon Gernon. I have often heard her say, "There is a difference between privacy and secrecy." I love leaning on that when I want something kept private. But I'm never sure what to do with it when I want to keep something secret. I don't trust anyone who says they have no secrets. I believe there is indeed a righteous minority who have lived shockingly pure lives—but even they have secrets. Even if those secrets have lived no farther than their own minds.

The little boy's determination bought him more time than any other child received on Santa's knee. And he used it wisely. Clever boy. I remember feeling so proud of him for seizing the opportunity and chancing the occasion. Some of us spend our entire lives second-guessing and squandering opportunities that may never come back.

He sat up straight, exhaled larger than life, squeezed me and chirped, *"Multumesc"* (thank you). Then he bounced off my lap, gathered his gifts and returned to his buddies. I watched them giggle and gasp while poking through their gift bags. Liberated for at least a few happy minutes by speaking his truest heart and finding out the world didn't end when he did.

Mos Craciun was pooped by the time the very last child had his picture taken. And with a booming *"Craciun fericit!"* (Merry Christmas), he vanished from the hall.

I sat in the administrator's office too physically and emotional exhausted to change right away. I could hear the orphanage staff calling out instructions back in the dining hall, gathering children into dorm groups and preparing them to leave.

Mere seconds later, I could hear the children outside on the pathways, lugging their wares through the heavy fog, back to rooms with no mommies or daddies ready to kiss them goodnight.

It was a special night for the children, if for no other reason than because it was not the norm. It was an overwhelming night for our faithful team as we were all turned inside out with emotion, once again. It was an inspired night because the young Romanian volunteers, who would return to serve on less eventful occasions long after we departed, were brilliant. But for me, all these descriptors fail in depicting what the night really was.

Beyond the darkness of territorial Santa legends that include dismemberment, the history of a nation with decades of healing to go before they can even start to imagine prosperity, the endless childhood communities of abandonment, and a fraudulent soda pop Santa without a clue—it was a night when none of it could rob a beautiful little boy brave enough to *carpe diem* (seize the day).

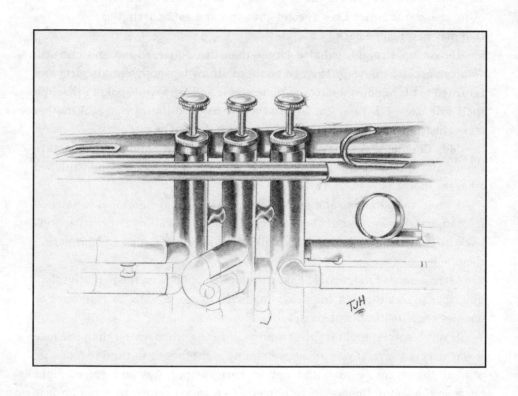

Here comes the question. You can sit still and answer it. You can get up and look around as you answer it. But you must begin answering the question as soon as you have read it. Furthermore, everything in your answer, all together, must fit into a single backpack. Before you read any farther, if you're up for the full impact of the exercise, you may even want to get a backpack and take it on as a two-minute challenge. However you approach it, you're on the clock with only 120 seconds. Read no farther until your pair of minutes have expired.

Ready?

Go.

Question: Believing that you would never return to your home again, and would never be able to retrieve anything you leave behind, if you literally had two minutes to gather the things that are most important to you and stuff them into a backpack—essentials, valuables, keepsakes—what would you take?

Now that your two minutes are done, take as long as you need to consider what you took. Why you took it. What you missed, how you missed it and how you will do without it.

And then meet Bronty.

Bronty was a pit bull of a boy. His walk was menacing, his voice was gravel filled, and he sneered like Clint Eastwood in all of his most memorable movie clips. Tattoos rose above his collar, painting his throat, and bled below his sleeves onto the backs of his hands. Piercings of small bullets and hooks covered his face. All of this nuancing his boldest street-fashion statement—a fascination with skulls and the punk, heavy metal and hardcore bands that used them as icons. From Iron Maiden's skeletal band mascot "Eddie" to the "Fiend Skull" of the iconic punk band the Misfits, angry and bloodied skull patches and ink markings adorned Bronty from head to toe. He was a Halloween terror to behold.

But it was misrepresentation by optic association at its peak. At the end of the day, he simply did anything and everything to become the boy nobody would mess with. And few did.

However, not only did most people not want to mess with him, most didn't even want to come near him. And even the hardcore of the hardcore on the streets kept a self-imposed other-side-of-the-street rule of thumb. Not because Bronty looked like a monster and acted like a madman, but because he looked like a monster and was silent and slow moving like a cat on the prowl. Bronty had learned to turn his authentic quiet demeanour into a menacing form of self-defence. One that allowed him to see everyone and be touched and known by no one.

From the outside of street life looking in (as ironic as that statement is), most people think that sympathy should be the order of the day for the do-or-die street dweller. If people feel sorry for you, surely they will be more charitable. Panhandling with matted hair sprouting from beneath a ratty toque is much more profitable than doing it with bright blue spiked hair. The odds on revenue while holding out a coffee cup are much higher while wearing a soiled trench coat than they are in a detailed leather jacket.

North American films are riddled with cues for living out a make-believe "Lifestyles of the Poor and Homeless." And they seldom include the have-nots having anything more than a dirty blanket, half a thrown-away sandwich and a mysterious bottle in a brown bag. There are generic standards for everything. We want our sports heroes and movie stars to be larger than life, our dream houses to have white picket fences, our laundry to be lemony fresh and our homeless people to look homeless.

While Bronty was the polar opposite to the standards set for a Homelessness 101 grad, he was the gold standard for surviving the untold story of homelessness after midnight. His past as he'd survived it, his present as he viewed it, and his future as he could best guess it were all hinged on a single word.

Safety.

When all the tourists and sightseers were tucked in, watching HBO in hotel rooms, when all the executives and store owners had finished working extra hours, when all the skyscrapers and malls had locked doors, and when no more subway trains were felt rumbling beneath the exhaust grates—there was another world of homelessness to navigate. One that mattered much more to a boy with the appearance of a vulture and the heart of a dove. One that rode the scars on his body, the scars in his heart, the scars in his mind and the scars in his soul. And so Bronty became like a monster to protect himself from all the other monsters.

I spent months trying to break his code of complete mistrust. Small human-being gestures that initially made him scowl and growl at me eventually began to defrost his cold charade. Simple things like standing at a normal distance for a conversation, looking him in the eyes and asking follow-up questions to one-word responses and grunts.

It took six entire months to get to the place of asking him the one question I really wanted to ask. I knew I would only get one chance and that rushing my question would squander the opportunity. One that I knew would reveal his true identity and open up doors that I guessed even he thought had been shut, locked and barricaded forever. Not a direct question about his ex-home, family or history. But a question that I had a sense would eventually allow him to pour out some of the cement weighing down his soul. And while I was correct about what the question might do, I never imagined where it would lead.

I began asking him about the patches and doodles on his jacket and backpack, purposefully not moving directly to the one that interested me most. We back and forthed about the various icons of violence, anarchy and brutality, blood and bone emblems for underground cult bands and logos for edgy mainstream acts. His uniform was an impressive montage of ghoulish favour, but for one glaring exception—the item that Bronty would not leave behind in his own two-minute scramble to leave home forever.

Safety-pinned to a side flap on his backpack was a small yellow happy-face patch with block letters around its circumference that read "God Made Me Special." While all of the larger patches had just two safety pins securing them, this small patch had four. It could not be risked. Too important.

"So what's with this one?" I asked as unassumingly as I could, while tapping the happy face between the eyes.

He opened his mouth to speak, then stopped himself before he did. He looked down at the patch, then back at me, then down at the ground.

"Nothing. Never mind. Doesn't matter," he mumbled.

But I had waited too long for a never-mind answer and knew I would only get one shot.

"C'mon, what? Of all the stuff attached to you, I think this one is by far the most interesting," I fake laughed.

He leaned against the graffiti-stained wall for several minutes, looking at the ground. And I said nothing as the question sat fat between us. Bronty kicked the dirt at his feet and sighed several times. I knew he was at war with himself—allied forces saying, "Attack!" Enemy forces saying, "Retreat!" Desperate to both tell and not tell.

Finally, he looked up. "Do you really give a damn?"

Instantly, I felt sick about the laughing tone of my "c'mon" prodding.

"Yes, I really do."

In tones so low that I had to lean in closer than natural for a conversation—and no doubt, closer than anyone had stood near Bronty in ages—he shared the story of the mystery patch.

When Bronty was eight years old, his best friend, Tommy, lived two doors down on the same side of the street. Tommy's family was quite involved in a small, friendly church in their community. The summer that Bronty was to turn nine, Tommy's mom offered to bring Bronty along with Tommy to a week-long summer day camp happening at the church. Bronty's mom and dad didn't care either way and were just glad he was out of their way. So Bronty went. There were lots of games, fun songs, crafts, simple Bible lessons. Standard fare from good church folk for community kids on summer vacation.

Bronty was able to carry the story this far without hesitation. His voice never rose or fell, but just hummed through all the details. Until he reached this sentence:

"And there was this little old lady..."

And it cracked. But it didn't feel like just his voice cracked. It felt like his heart cracked. It felt like the shell around him cracked. It felt like all the monsters he was trying to attach himself to cracked.

I stood silent in those cracks and waited for whatever might come next. And there in his eyes was the one thing he had spent every ounce of his energy fighting.

Fear.

Bronty had been able to build a defensive system against all the physical fears of the street, but not against those that aren't afraid of scary pictures of skulls and ice-cold sneers. The fear of hurt. The fear of caring. The fear of remembering. And most of all, the fear of trusting.

Fears that make Bronty like everyone else. Fears that make him much more similar than different from clean-cut kids from decent homes, getting good grades. Fears that many people carry all the way to the grave.

He cleared his throat several times in an effort to compose himself and continue. But each time his voice gave way, and soon the look in his eyes turned from fear to complete panic. There was a little boy still inside, terrified to be seen. No different than the harmless little old man behind the curtain manning all the levers and knobs that made the great Wizard of Oz bellow and blow smoke.

"It's okay." I wanted to say more but knew that saying too much was too high a gamble.

He took a giant breath, puffed his cheeks, and exhaled.

"Damn you!" he snorted, and continued by taking a different tact at getting it out. "What the f*ck! You wanna know? Okay, fine. Here it is..."

Reverting to his harsh street corner tenor, he launched into the end of the story. Barely into his second sentence, the softness of the sacred moments remembered would not allow him to misrepresent them, and he continued, gradually, almost to a whisper.

The Monday to Friday camp started each day at 9 a.m. and ended at 4 p.m. But at 3:45 p.m., something special happened. More uplifting than the games, more interesting than the crafts, more joyous than the singing and more alive than the lessons. An old woman—who told the kids to call her "Grandma Lu"— would show up. There was a chair set up for her at the bottom of the steps outside the church's front doors. She would make her way up the front path using her walker and back herself into the chair. A camp helper would then come and set a small box on the little table beside her. And there she would sit, watching the kids and laughing, waiting for the final 15 minutes to lapse before her fleeting moments of sweet engagement.

Her task was simple. At the end of each day, the children would line up in front of her and she would hand out a small treat for the day. One day, it was a special pencil. Another, it was a multicoloured balloon. It was never anything grand. And it didn't need to be, because she had found a way to make all of it priceless.

Five days in a row, she would show up at 3:45 p.m. and wait with anticipation for a few moments of time to cherish the children. And on the last day, she tattooed a little boy's heart in a way that a lifetime of body art never will. At 4 p.m., on a sunny August afternoon, Grandma Lu gave Bronty just enough life to survive all the hell that was on its way.

She was handing out yellow happy-face patches. One at a time, she would take them out of the little box and make sure she rose to an occasion most people would offer up as insignificant. By Friday afternoon, she had memorized every name and could place it correctly with each little face. And when it was Bronty's turn, she held his open hand in hers, held up the patch with her other hand, and smiled. Then she placed the patch in his hand and wrapped both of hers around it—just like grandmas do when they're giving treat money for the corner store. She pulled him close and said, "Bronty, God made you special." Then she pulled his hand towards her and kissed it.

By the time Bronty was finished telling me the story, he was in tears. There weren't any tough guys, dark symbols or mean streets in that moment. Just a beautiful story. While he ran his finger across the embossed words on the patch, he squeezed out, "It's the only time I'd ever been told that."

Eight years later, Bronty's dad came home drunk one day from work. A day tragically like so many other days, but one that Bronty would make sure would end completely differently. Bronty's mom had left without a trace three years prior. Bronty and his mom had been victims of his father's constant beatings for years. Following in his mother's footsteps, having taken all the beatings and pain he could sustain, Bronty decided to vanish.

As he told it, "I knew I had two minutes to gather my things and get out the window before my dad stumbled up to my room." Two minutes of terror, confusion and adrenaline. And still, somehow in those dizzying seconds of panic, that patch made it into his highest priority list of things that could not be left behind.

It's a story hallmarked with a myriad of God-filled life lessons—the lasting impression of tenderness, the sustenance of kindness, the power of truth. But most of all, it's a grand commentary on excellence.

The prolific Greek philosopher Aristotle said, "We are what we repeatedly do. Excellence, then, is not an act, but a habit."

Grandma Lu couldn't run the rah-rah games, rein in a gang of kids for big-actions sing-songs, or prove herself as the life of the party. Those years had long passed her by. She could barely sustain the walk to the bottom of the front steps. But when it was her turn to do her part, she received the opportunity as a gift and treated it as such. She knew that a moment to cherish a child was a precious thing, not to be squandered. And her habit of excellence honoured that.

When I was in my first year of high school, I had a grade 9 music teacher who left an indelible impression on me. I played the trumpet and wasn't very good at it. Thus, I had been one of three students relegated to playing the third trumpet parts. And rightly so. During one morning band practice, Mr. J. broke down a 24-bar segment of a complex baroque aria to be played section by section so he could identify something that was sounding "off." When he got to the brass sections, he quickly identified something wrong in the trumpet section. So he broke it down further. The first trumpets played—the melodic lead, the dancing voice of the song. Then the second trumpets performed—harmonies bouncing in thirds below the leads, breaking midway into a counter-melody. And then the third trumpets were called into action. But this was on a morning when the two other horn players were away. And so, before the entire band, I played a solo of what I was sure was the most boring 24 bars of music ever written. Six consecutive, annoying, repetitive D whole notes.

D–2,3,4. D–2,3,4. D–2,3,4. D–2,3,4. D–2,3,4. D–2,3,4. It felt like it went on forever.

I played them one after the other with no enthusiasm, then rested the horn on my lap and rolled my eyes. And the room laughed. Mr. J. knew I was embarrassed by the redundant, skill-less task that was mine and kindly spoke directly to me by speaking to the entire class.

"No, no, no laughing. You see, class, those notes are holding it all together. They are the soil that all the other melodies grow in. This music is not complete without them."

He went on to tell the class that the band would never be at its best unless we all played our parts to the best of our ability and respected that no one's part was too small or insignificant. And just before counting the entire band back into bar one, Mr. J. looked at me, smiled, and said with astounding generosity, "Okay, great. Just need to remind you that all those beautiful long Ds should be D sharps." In my boredom, I had not bothered to check the key signature, and indeed, I had been the culprit holding 24 bars of the wrong note.

Grandma Lu no doubt had played many leads in her day among family, friends, community and co-workers. Likely some stunning harmonies and counter-melodies in the scheme of things too. But time and circumstance had caught up with her, and it was her turn to play the third trumpet parts in much of life. But she didn't roll her eyes and enter in haphazardly. Excellence in serving others was not her act—it was her habit. She knew that her best efforts created a fertile soil for beautiful melodies and brought excellence to the part many would've walked away from.

Three years, two prison stints, and four cities after I first met Bronty, he tracked me down at my office by phone. We talked for ten minutes at the most, but he wanted me to know he was starting all over—and that the only patch he was carrying was a yellow happy face.

If we look to the intellects to settle our minds, organize our thoughts and drive our convictions, we'll surely go mad.

Case in point:

Wander through the brains of renowned thinkers and speakers on the issue of patriotism. There are endless heavy-hearted contenders weighing in throughout history, ready to duke it out with endless commitment. Lace up the gloves on any two of them, drop them in the same ring, and you would have to guess their fighting styles would not change or adapt regardless of the opponent's.

Patriotism: devoted love, support, and defence of one's country; national loyalty.

In this corner, Irish playwright and accomplished orator George Bernard Shaw: "Patriotism is a pernicious, psychopathic form of idiocy."

And in this corner, twentieth-century U.S. Democratic presidential nominee and diplomat, noted for his intellectual demeanour, Adlai E. Stevenson: "Patriotism is not short, frenzied outbursts of emotion, but the tranquil and steady dedication of a lifetime."

Oh boy. Ding-ding.

And the only person leaving the ring concussed is anyone stuck in the middle who has not been aligned to one hardcore ideological corner or the other. People like me—dissed lightweights, lollygagging somewhere in the middle.

Stuck in the denial of middle-agedness, when you're supposed to have glued yourself to a few big picture ideologies, even now I find myself hiding comfortably behind a lovely middle-ground sentiment, compliments of the now-deceased, internationally renowned Spanish Catalan cellist Pablo Casals: "The love of one's country is a splendid thing. But why should love stop at the border?"

CHAPTER 5

I like everything about that statement.

One of the great surprises to my friends who exist outside of my "ministry" circles is that this is such a volatile dialogue inside of those circles. The truth is, I have given the discussion great thought. I have done my best to look at it through a global lens. And I have seen the end-game ravages of oppression instituted by way of war and the forced will of conquerors.

This neither debunks nor liberates me from the responsibility of my overly fortunate place in the world as a white Canadian male who never faced a military draft or spent a moment wondering if a bomb would steal my family. At the same time, I'm in many ways a product of the way I was raised, taught without question about taking pride in my nation and respecting the sacrifices made.

So rather than stake a claim on any extreme, I continue to listen closely, ask thoughtful questions, respect and enter the discussion, care deeply, love my country and not let it "stop at the border," and most of all, try not to lose my mind.

It was to, at, and from 502 Spadina Avenue in downtown Toronto on a cool Remembrance Day that I was pressed but one more time to muddle my mind's way through the murky water of patriotism, valour, associated sacrifice and the notion of a "just" war. Spadina, just north of College Street. The Scott Mission.

The Scott Mission in Toronto is one of the most storied refuge and relief missions in Canada. At age 17, having departed his homeland of Poland just before the First World War, Morris Zeidman stumbled across The Christian Synagogue in 1908, established by the Presbyterian Church in Canada—a vision realized by Rev. J. MacPherson Scott to minister to Jewish immigrants. Impacted by the synagogue's leadership, Morris embraced Christianity and went on to be ordained. Upon Rev. Scott's death in 1920, the synagogue was renamed the Scott Institute in his honour, and Morris gave leadership to the broadening of its outreach, to serve poor people from any background. By the time the Great Depression arrived, the Scott Institute was serving as many as 1,000 people per day.

As his passion and vision grew, by the end of 1941, during the height of the Second World War, Morris, with wife Annie at his side, founded the Scott Mission as an independent, non-denominational mission. Seventy years later, their services include daily hot meals, a clothing bank, groceries, showers and laundry facilities for homeless people, an overnight program, shelter, visitation for shut-ins, low-cost daycare, and after-school children and youth programs and summer camps.

While much of what "the Scott" has done, or does, is richly purposed, it is not necessarily novel. Sadly, by necessity, North America is significantly dotted with missions for the poor, large and small, lifting the mantle of service, grace and benevolence. I have entered the doors of a great many of them and seen the distressing and all-too-familiar sights of food lines, drop-in lines, shelter lines, and line-ups for every other basic necessity imaginable. If there is one thing "the poor" know well, it's lining up.

But one November 11th, I caught wind of something I hadn't seen or heard of before. A Remembrance Day service in honour of homeless veterans. The notion of it stirred me instantly, and I knew I had to be there.

The Scott Mission is situated in a very interesting location, at the north tip of one of the largest Chinatown communities in all of North America. More than a century old, Toronto's Chinatown is a growing community that was forced to relocate several times due to municipal development and expropriation, landing where it is decades after the founding of the Scott Mission.

Parking is an issue anywhere in Toronto's downtown core, so when I find a spot within a reasonable walking distance, I take it, disinterested in the guesswork or hope required for finding something better. In fact, accounting for the midday hustle and bustle of Canada's busiest metropolis, on these occasions I will park an unreasonable walking distance away, just happy knowing I won't get snagged by ticket or tow.

And so I did. Just outside Golden Leaf Chinese Cuisine. A 20-minute walk—minimum—to the mission. I squeezed into a tiny spot on the main street with an inch-by-inch, 20-point parallel park, proud of my unlikely accomplishment, and raced to the automated parking meter to pay my dues.

Between my vehicle and the machine sat a hacking beggar. Of course, I simply mean a sickly person who was panhandling. But at the very moment I noticed her, a disgruntled businessman accidentally passed by her too close for his own comfort as she choked up a wad of phlegm at his feet, and he shouted at the top of his lungs, "Damn you, hacking beggar!" And so it stuck, from the moment I saw her. As repulsed as I was by the cruelty of it all, the words were plastered on my brain—*hacking beggar.*

And truly, while words like "beggar," "tramp" and "bum" make my stomach turn, "hacking" she was. She processed a relentless bark of a cough, hoarse enough that just the sound of it alone was painful.

She was young. Very young. Too young to survive the streets for any length of time without being rapidly sucked into the vortex of its unforgiving culture. The kind of fresh-faced youth that sets off any semi-experienced outreach worker with panic. She sat wide-eyed and sickly on a pad of laminated card-board sheets, with an empty Styrofoam take-out container at her feet, wishing on spare change. As I hi-ed and smiled in my hurry, I saw but a single silver quarter in her vacant tub.

Debit, credit and the drive to a cashless society have sullied a beggar's cause, regardless of hacks, snorts, sniffles, stinks or otherwise. Where the introduction of the Canadian one dollar coin upped a panhandler's ante in 1987, by the time the Canadian two dollar coin was released in 1996, Interac direct payment by debit card was the most popular purchase method in the country. Even I was literally penniless while swiping my ten dollar meter payment.

I weaved through the crowded and mysterious ethnic enclave the same way I had for years. Intrigued by the walkway madness over everything from medicinal herbs to handmade clothing, and mystified by the sights of marinated meats and fish parts I could not identify. A 20-minute hike past more unpackaged and open-air food than anywhere else in the country, leading to the front doors of one of the nation's largest missions, filled with hungry people. Sometimes the greatest and strangest paradoxes of all are the ones we don't recognize.

As far as I was concerned, the mission's Remembrance Day service was excellent. A sensitive but unashamed tact on patriotism gave centre stage to the best intentions of "honouring" individuals lost through the cracks of time. Perhaps, even if the only one, the place even the most ardent pacifist might give credence to military remembrance. For honouring is often the only lifeboat from grief. And the grief of losing loved ones to any sort of plight, predicament or cause, agreeable or not, is the narrow gateway of sameness to all humanity.

I left with a heavy heart. And rightly so. For at the centre of ceremony was homage to "the walking wounded." A population both uncounted and unaccounted for. Those who had fought for the convictions of their hearts and have no place to lay their heads. Those who found valour in youth and disregard in age. Those who sacrificed in combat boots and are sacrificed to second-hand shoes. Those who survived the trenches and now brave the gutters. Those who lost friends on the front lines, limbs on the battlefield and minds on the minefield. Those who believed in a just war and have been shown no justice. My heart was heavy, poised for even more than remembrance for the fallen but imagining the dream of reconciliation for the living. And honour for the walking wounded.

Lost in my thoughts, the weave and bob of my return walk was interrupted just shy of my parking spot. For there sat a fragile man who had not been there 90 minutes prior. A faint and unattended skeleton of a man, lost beneath a lop-sided beret, with a tiny leather satchel in his lap. The unassuming face of the ceremony's voice, quelled to the margins and completely unaware. I stopped at a distance and reached in my pockets, dashed by the convenience of plastic cards.

As I drew near and took a knee, I saw from the corner of my eye the hacking beggar pass by and enter a store fronted by dragons. I thought little of it, but for the guess she would get the boot if she was spotted before she reached the restroom.

The small, thin relic was hard to understand as I gave chat my best shot. Denture free, he was more bottom lip than face. But we carried on a wee bit as I tried to share the gist and solemnity of where I'd just been. He smiled and nodded, without giving away whether unimpressed or understanding.

For better or worse, or whatever peculiar state treads water in between, I am an easily-lit cherry bomb when it comes to are-you-kidding-me street patrons. I would've thought the seemingly endless curbside years would have muted that emotional response, but they never have. If I see a homeless teen carrying a baby on the street, I am all about street moms and street babies. Until I see an amputee panning from a wheelchair, when I become all about handicaps and homelessness. So on this day, if I had been carrying a soapbox, all of Chinatown would've taken a serious earful. It's not a smart response, allows for little peace, and over time can cause even the best of friends to tune out. But I have made peace with it and have learned to measure my responsive outpour, while thanking the good Lord that my blood can still simmer, if not boil.

Just as I shifted knees, a shadow fell before me. I heard a husky throat clear and peered up. Flanking my nearside was the hacking beggar, brown and red paper lantern-bag in hand. She paid me no mind, as though I were invisible. She bent before the old man, opened the bag, and spread chicken and noodles before him as though a feast for the king. I froze stone-cold still. Finally, she looked at me, smiled, and propped up a small face-down sign that I had not noticed.

"War Veteran. God bless."

She stood, turned, and walked away, hacking as though her lungs were ready to pop out.

Honour.

This story is not about war. Nor is it about patriotism. It requires no debate, and I would spend not a moment on it. This story is about the cost of honouring. A cost too expensive for most to assume. A cost that takes no credit but humility and offers no refund but sacrifice.

Tradition has it that we honour mildly at birthdays. Cake, candles, and the most uncreative lyrics to a four-line ditty ever written usually do the trick. Usually gifts when we're young or something a bit meatier when hitting a milestone year that ends with o. But in general, the only multigenerational, multi-cultural, multi-economic honouring that North Americans play into across the board is purposed around notice of a calendar date.

Weddings take an angle on it, and retirements might catch a whiff, but for the most part, for any real bent on honouring someone it takes a good funeral to get it right. And even then, it's there that we repeatedly trip over the obvious tragedy of our traditions, take little notice and keep on keepin' on. "Today, we don't want to grieve the loss of *so-and-so* but celebrate *so-and-so's* life."

I wonder if that's what God wants from us. I'm sure the goodness in our hearts is pleasing, but it must be incredibly sad that His children can't seem to pick up on the obvious. Ah, what it would sound like if we really knew when and how to honour one another!

"Today, we grieve big time, because we are sooooooo going to miss all the great celebrating of *so-and-so's* life we did at their side."

Honouring a life as it's lived rather than short-changing it as a memory. Imagine all the regrets we would do without.

It need not be pomp and circumstance. Sans regalia, void of pageantry, spectacle annulled. To truly honour, or be honoured, has as much to do with marching bands and long speeches as it does with kway teow noodles and chicken balls. For at the centre of all upright honouring is but a single core merit.

Respect.

Where there is no respect, there can be no honour. Where there is no honour, there can be no celebration. Where there is no celebration, there can be no belonging.

How can it be that, while it all but flies over mainstream heads, a hacking beggar would know it so?

Too few distractions? Enough time to reflect? Liberation from ambition? Reverence for life? Respect for small acts of kindness? Whatever it is, whatever glorious combination of soul shakers fuse, consistently, it is modelled nowhere greater than among the poorest of the poor.

As I drove away, the aged soldier sat alone with his lunch, compliments of but one more dubious angel. The cherub of esteem. The seraph of honour.

Be assured: we walk among angels.

"It is not our purpose to become each other; it is to recognize each other, to learn to see the other, and honour him for what he is"–Hermann Hesse, impassioned German-born Swiss poet, novelist and painter.

It's no wonder I struggled with math all through school. I don't like numbers. An aversion to numbers may sound like a strange thing, but I've got stranger quirks than that. We all do. And if examined closely enough, no matter how preposterous, they usually make some sense.

It's easy in North America to assume that full kitchen cupboards represent full stomachs. But seldom is it considered that empty shelves might signify much more than empty tummies. The likes of World Vision faithfully teach us, inspire us, and invite us all to a grander understanding and participation around global hunger and development. A legacy without bounds. And still, faint is our widespread social capacity to recognize a tangible like food as more than just food. Especially in our own backyards.

An industrialized addiction to numbers often prevents us from looking deeply into the human nuances of our own communities. Stuck in the rut of relying on raw data to guide our opinions, decisions and responses, and all too often paving the way for our ultimate neglect. While statistics are built as gauges for accuracy, they can also numb us to recognizing the details that matter most. Details that numbers in neat little columns cannot measure. Information of the soul that doesn't simply compute by input and tally. The cost of tears. The expense of shame. And the price of hope. It shouldn't take a team of researchers to know how our neighbours are. And certainly, we have a supernatural source telling us *who* they are.

A total stranger, simply sharing the same sidewalk bench. As everyday an occurrence as happens, well...every day. But it was 20 minutes that changed me in ways I cannot fully explain.

I didn't realize that she was crying until after several minutes at her side. Sheepishly, she did all she could to conceal it. But a sniffle betrayed her, and I looked her way.

"Sorry," she whispered, inexplicably.

From word one, she broke my heart. That she thought the interruption of a sniffle should require an apology was profoundly telling.

"It's okay," I nodded ridiculously, recognizing instantly how foolishly the brain can react.

It's okay? Ugh. What—that she needed to apologize for sniffling? That I wasn't too bothered by the inconvenience? Or how about the fact that my pedestrian existence in the moment held no weight against her clear anguish? I wanted to instantly follow up with the opposite of "It's okay," but the obvious reversal—"It's not okay"—sure wasn't right.

So I proceeded with the next worst thing. "You okay?"

Sigh. Clearly not.

Graciously, she grinned through her tears. "No. I guess not."

She watched me from the corner of her eye—opening my mouth, then stopping myself several times, lost in the overwhelming desire not to say anything dumber than I already had in just four words. She wiped her cheeks and bravely proceeded to put us both out of our awkward misery.

"If I could just go in and..." She left the moment hanging and began to cry again.

Her name was Teresa.

We were sitting in front of a small local food bank, in the west end of the city. One by one, people entered the side doors inconspicuously, departing with a few paper sacks or small cardboard boxes minutes later. I had just accepted a volunteer position on the board of directors for the Daily Bread Food Bank—an organization that serves almost 80,000 people in the Greater Toronto Area through a network of 160 member agencies and over 190 food relief programs. Incredible numbers as numbers go. But their further mandates were even more intriguing to me—to mobilize greater community and corporate support, involvement and action, and to create social change to reduce poverty through research, education and advocacy. Impressive goals.

This modest little food bank was one of our member agencies. Staffed predominantly, as is always the case, with unpretentious volunteers. Most of them senior citizens, maintaining the sad but true status quo of which generation is able to faithfully serve in the most thankless of ways. I was touring a few community-based food banks to get a better sense of what all the big numbers boiled down to. And at the end of the day, for me, it was all about Teresa. And it still is.

I presumed she was too embarrassed to bring herself to ask for food. I was wrong. Par for the course on my never-ending and humbling learning curve.

I gave her my best "It's okay" and "I understand" smile. It wasn't and I didn't, but it was all I had to offer. She sighed and dropped her head, too weary to appease my feeble attempts.

We sat silently for the most eternal 30 seconds I can remember, until I said with makeshift confidence, "It's okay. Lots of people need the help. No need to be ashamed."

To this day, I cannot recall stringing together all the wrong words so proficiently or efficiently.

We sat in another 30 seconds of embarrassed hush, until I broke it with one final loose cannon.

"Seriously."

Enough was enough. She cleared her throat and swallowed, then tilted her head toward me and looked me in the eyes for the first time.

"I was just there yesterday," she surrendered softly.

I dropped my shoulders and pinched out my first decent word of the day. "Sorry."

And she understood. It was one of those juicy, plump sorries that plop down, wiggle around and spread slowly, oozing over acres of soulful real estate. The kind of sorry she had known only too well. I knew by the expression on her face that the tone of my voice unpacked my sorry. Sorry that I didn't even have the chance to misunderstand because I was too busy drawing conclusions. Sorry that she had to explain her pain to a total stranger to get a moment's peace. Sorry that the big story that bruised her was filled with an immense sorrow I had no right to tap on. And most of all, sorry that I am a fool.

But it was also the kind of sorry God likes to use when He creates moments that you can't see coming.

She bit her bottom lip and rubbed her eyes. Then she began to speak, privileging me with her story, by beginning with the ageless words spoken by would-be poverty survivors around the world and throughout history: "If only..."

And so her sad story began at the end, "if only-ed" at the prospect of a few more groceries, then backtracking into both the complex and minor details that always criss-cross and bob below the surface of every life story.

This day's urgency was all about stocked shelves. Not for the sake of hunger—she was long past overcoming those pains—but for the sake of optics. Teresa was teetering on the last-chance tightrope of parental scrutiny. Children's Aid was looking for evidence of adequate care for her children, and Teresa was certain that her barren cupboards would further implicate her as unfit. She'd spent the past several days scrubbing floors and walls until her hands were raw and doing laundry in the bathtub. She stole toilet paper and light bulbs from public restrooms, condiments and napkins from fast-food joints, and flowers from the front garden of the library. Her children had been removed from the home months prior, and Teresa had not been able to prove herself fit for their return. She was terrified that she was running out of chances.

She was five minutes into her story at the most when she lost me. Just for a few moments. But as critical a few moments as I'd had since childhood. Just long enough to feel the pangs of something I hadn't felt in a long time. Teresa commented that the wheels fell off when she had a nervous breakdown and could not pull herself out from the ensuing depression that came with it. And even as she told it, I was swallowed into the vortex of painful recollection and buried emotions. Her words kept coming. But I was not there. I was eight years old again.

In the autumn of 1972, my own mother had a nervous breakdown and fell into an incapacitating depression for several months. She would stay in her room, in the dark, for days at a time. My father was heroic in working long hours at his blue collar job all week long, looking after his three sons in the evenings and on weekends, and still leading a community outreach for boys in the local church. All while tending to his wife in her indescribable turmoil. Through God's patchwork of my dad's unconditional love, the support and prayers of loved ones, the counsel of doctors, and her eventual realization and coming to grips with the fact that she was angry at God for pains she'd suffered decades earlier, my mom eventually found enough courage for the uphill climb to wellness. The same courage evidenced in her permitting me to share her story here, so that others might have hope.

The term "nervous breakdown" is not a medical term, nor a technically subscribed psychiatric disorder. And depression is one of the most contentious diseases in modern history. But one thing is certain. While variances in diagnosis and manifestation are broad, guesswork and skepticism make it no less real, and no less debilitating.

John D. Halliwell wrote for the Canadian Mental Health Association (May 1, 2001), "For the depressive, there is a total dissolution of the thin distancing line between their own melancholic reality and the condition of the outside world. All aspects of life seem to be one endless tragedy to a distorted mind that is falling into a deep mental depression."

But all the detailed analysis in the world doesn't amount to much for a little boy who just wants Mommy to be Mommy again. Nothing is more profound in its simplicity than the mind of a child. What I remember most is negotiating the two top steps of our staircase. They were right outside my parents' room. The two-inch hardwood slats in the floor had loosened over time, and they would creak when stepped on. During the months of her despair, I was always afraid of disturbing my mom and whatever else loomed behind her bedroom door, so I would try and step over the noisy stairs by leaning off the baseboard, angling myself against the railing and sliding myself down to the third step. Coming back up, I would shimmy against the railing and crawl over the top post. For me, the greatest indicator at the time, and tender memory now, of my mom's healing came when I could let those stairs creak again.

I will never forget one day in particular. Moments of peace and quiet joy that I couldn't even identify with words until now. My mom was cooking supper in our small kitchen. It had been a long time since that had occurred. The smell of pork chops wafted up the stairwell where I stood facing the blue sky window opposite the landing, rocking back and forth on the top stair, while its familiar squeak sang out that my mommy was okay.

It was this ironic recollection of food on the kitchen table that woke me and returned me to Teresa. Food that had meant more than just food. Teresa continued with her own story, unaware that I had been absent, passing by monumental pains with fleeting words.

"When the father of my children walked out..."

"I've been three months clean and sober..."

"I didn't know my own dad..."

In ten minutes, she breezed over baggage that would take decades of professional help to unpack. But she just moved it out of the way quickly, ending her story by apologizing for inconveniencing me with a few minutes of listening. Which even then, I had done poorly. Only then did I notice that she was holding a picture of her children between her palms.

"Can I see that?" I nodded towards her hands.

She held the picture in front of me, too sacred to hand it over.

"Beautiful," I offered.

"Yes, beautiful," she replied, holding the picture against her chest.

She looked up at the food bank door and said with a long exhale, "They aren't allowed to give you food two days in a row, y'know."

She continued by tearing out my heart with "I could actually bring it back. I just need to borrow it."

Borrowing food for appearance. Appearance to bring back children. Children to restore worth. Worth to bring life. Life to restore confidence.

Confidence to move forward. Forward to possibility. Possibility to bring home food. Food to keep. The cycle, next to impossible to succeed, was both ridiculous and tragic. And still, watching her gather the courage to attempt it was extraordinary.

I could bear no more. I leaned away from her to reach into my back pocket, to pull out my wallet. No sooner had I done so than she stood and was on her way. She went for it the way children do off a diving board the first time. Thinking about it, almost doing it, getting close, losing nerve, thinking about it again, trying not to think about it...and finally, just doing it.

I wanted to call out, "No, no, come back!" But her courage peaked and her esteem needed nothing less than my pity.

Monitoring food sharing in small community food banks is no easy task. "Sharing the wealth" (to suggest the most ironic of metaphors) is complex. Case in point: Even in the first visit the day before, did Teresa fit the profile of a single adult, or the parent of two? The answer could only have been known by looking into the near future. Further, "double dipping" is simply a no-no. But most double-dippers in the system would try separate food banks back-to-back, rather than pleading their case at the same one. Her chances at success were nil as far as I was concerned. Skeptics often call the whole system flawed. Many hard-working nine-to-fivers consider the whole thing a vice for scammers too lazy to get up and work.

But they are wrong. The system is not perfect, and never can be. It can be refined and tweaked and juiced by best practices, but it will always be as imperfect as the human condition. And so it should be. It only stands to reason that it will also be just as thoughtful and grace filled. The way any of us should hope and pray it is.

What needs to be respected most is that the people who lead food banks and meal programs, serve at them and give to them, are doing their best. They are not stupid. Their hearts are compassionate, but their psyches want no more to be duped than do those of the cynics'.

"Give us this day our daily bread" is no different a request of God for the rich than it is for the poor. Only pride and thanklessness confuse blessing with entitlement.

I sat on the bench alone for ten more minutes, my eyes fixed on the food bank entrance. Cowardly, I was debating leaving, fearful of witnessing her sad return, when the door slowly inched open. Teresa. Weighed down by two heavy plastic bags in each hand, she used her shoulder to press her way through. She bounced towards me, grinning from ear to ear.

"Look! Look! And I can keep them!" she marvelled.

She rested her cellophane packages and cans on the bench and chatted for another minute while struggling to find her bus fare. Then she gathered her bags and turned. No goodbye, just time to depart.

Five or six steps away, she turned back and, for whatever reason, said in a big happy voice, "I was named after Mother Teresa, y'know."

She twisted back and rushed away.

While there was wonder in those moments, I remained on the bench for some time, perplexed by the master plan. I sat alone, watching person after person come and go from the food bank. In with nothing. Out with something. Never enough, but more than they had minutes prior. Each one with a story as unique as Teresa's.

What plausible celebration was truly to be had? Kids can't go home to stolen bathroom tissue and food for show. I was never too lost in the moment to recognize that the truth was stacked against her. In fact, perhaps if she hadn't received the extra food, all the rightest things would have occurred, setting in motion a more sensible sequence of events. Children remain in safer environments? More time for Mom to regroup? Healthy options to unfold over time?

But faith doesn't work that way. Neither does prayer. And while the hand of God is impossible to understand, the love He shows through tender and broken hearts is the stuff that keeps the Teresas of this world afloat. And my mom. And me.

And so I am pressed against what I do know—that while I may not comprehend His resolve, God hears my prayers. That I can celebrate the soft heart of the one who dared to bend food bank rules by virtue of a listening ear and compassionate heart. And that maybe—just maybe—Teresa's tenacity on that day was the new start she needed.

But what I am most certain of is this. There is more than meets the eye in a well-stocked refrigerator or a plateful of hot food. There is something sweet about pouring ketchup from a bottle. There is much to be celebrated in the smell of clean laundry, warm from the dryer. There is light of a different kind behind bulbs that aren't burnt out. There is a legacy of wellness in naming our children well. And—without question—there is joy in the sound of creaking stairs.

Somewhere around week three of our prenatal classes, we were shown a film that would outline all the things we should think through and organize in preparation for the fast-approaching day of delivery. Some of it was common sense, some of it was solid advice, and all of it was a bit like make-believe for me, as I could barely comprehend any of what was going on, or what was to come. I am hard pressed to recall much of anything from those weeks of classes many years ago, let alone from that film, except for one piece of advice that literally made me laugh out loud.

The actors in the film performed all the staged calm and unrushed preparations for the big day the same fraudulent way the actors do in the if-the-airplane-goes-down emergency clips that kick off passenger flights. No panicking, no anxiety. Just a few mild-mannered instructions to survive the whole ordeal.

"Have the new-mom-to-be's overnight suitcase packed and ready at the door for when the time comes."

Okay, sure. Will do.

"Have the phone numbers in hand of those you will want to contact from the hospital."

Yep, good plan.

"Remember this. Do that. And don't forget this other thing."

And then it came. What I thought was the strangest bit of instruction I could ever have imagined: "And partners, don't forget to have a sandwich prepared and wrapped in the fridge to grab on the way out the door," and a long explanation that we might get hungry if the labour takes a long time and that the hospital cafeteria may be closed.

"Wow," I blurted out loud, "a guy must have made this movie."

I was just in the greatest of disbelief that while my spouse was going through the unimaginable pain of childbirth, and as a miracle was occurring before my eyes, I would actually take the time to lunch a bit. And if the whole thing did become a marathon, surely just sneaking off to a vending machine seemed less narcissistic than actually packing my very own brown bag in advance.

Well, when the day came, we walked through the hospital doors at 10 a.m. And a mere five hours later, we were holding our beautiful, healthy, 6 pound 8 ounce Sarah Jane.

Beautiful, right?

Yeah, for the most part. Except that by 11:30 a.m. (only an hour and a half after we'd arrived and not even real-life lunch time yet), all I could think about was how much I wished I'd done that sandwich thing. Believe it or not, at some point between my wife's wincing in pain and sucking on ice chips, I had even lost my mind enough to tell her so.

At around 6 p.m., Diane fell asleep with our tiny daughter in her arms, and I departed. And, well, I went straight to a burger joint.

The truth is for me, the whole post-hospital fast-food experience on that special day is an important part of the story. When I left my lovely wife and daughter in peaceful slumber, I really wasn't very hungry at all. Hmph, I don't think I ever really was on that day. More likely, it was just that that nutty movie had become stuck in my craw and temporarily brainwashed me. At least I like telling myself that. At any rate, I didn't know what else to do or where else to go. So that's where I went.

I couldn't believe that people were ordering food and sitting down to eat the way they always did. While driving there, I felt the same disbelief watching people pumping gas into their cars, entering banks and supermarkets, and reading newspapers at bus stops. Didn't they know that the whole world was different now? That a radical miracle had just occurred, and my life would be changed forever? And still, people were asking to supersize French fry orders, fumbling for change, and trying to use outdated coupons like it was any old normal day!

I wanted to scream at them. Every single one of them. Make them wake up! Give them the dutiful life-and-death yell: "Hey, hey, hey, all of you! Pay close attention and understand! You can't just act like everything is the same as it's always been! It's not!"

Yeah, the life-and-death yell. The one no one ever really lets loose, but the one we all scream inside our heads at the world when either life or death occurs intimately, and we watch outsiders go about their business as usual.

The joy of life and the grief of death. So diametrically opposed, yet conjuring up so many similar sensations for the soul. And none more vibrant than the mind-boggling comprehension of God. When it goes as hoped, it is so easy for believers to praise God for the start of healthy new life and the end of a long life well lived. And most often, a jolt of the same occurs for God-wonderers and even God-deniers in the same situations, as the miracles of life and death are just plain too mesmerizing not to at least ponder the supernatural and release credit for more than the human mind—or heart—can process.

But when it doesn't go "right," when the earth-shattering rip-off of less than the way we dreamt it occurs, when God has appeared to pitch easy lob balls to most people and impossible curveballs to you, praise to God—or any notion of deity—seems absurd. There's not a human alive—saint, scoundrel, or anything in-between—who hasn't felt they've been left to twist in the wind at some point over God's "rightness" in these matters.

I had a friend who lost twin baby girls, and with them her own desire to live. In her unimaginable loss and pain, she bounced between hating God and denying God, by the second. And still, she begged me to never stop assuring her of the one thing I told her I absolutely believed: that her babies were resting in the arms of God, waiting to meet her there one day. I will not spend a moment believing anything less, and will never be convinced otherwise. And while she laid claim to hatred and denial of God, at her core neither would she.

I can't imagine there is any painful twisting that is more excruciating than that of those who endure these divergent experiences of life and death at the same time.

We took our daughter home from the hospital the day after she was born. I wasn't really ready for that. Diane was calm, ready and eager. But I was sure somehow they had made too many assumptions about my capabilities, and, though mommy and baby were fine, that I should be tested and monitored before we brought the whole matter home. My biggest concern was always—and only—me. I had spent too much time making fun of those prenatal movies and not enough time paying attention. I didn't know how tight I could hold my baby girl. I thought every time she cried, it was because I was surely doing something very wrong. And the whole fontanelle thing had me completely freaked out, terrified I would inadvertently poke right through the top of her head at any given moment.

It was all a mystery to me. All these years later, it still very much is.

As we departed, we passed a large plate glass window outside the nurses' station, behind which the newborns who weren't ready to go home were sleeping. Wee bundled beauties in little caps, with giant tubes and wires connecting them to beeping machines and monitors many sizes bigger than the actual babies, while their little bodies struggled to take big wheezy breaths. Why was my baby leaving in such a hurry, having had no mechanical hook-ups, while moms and dads peered through glass windows at their babies in teary-eyed uncertainty?

That moment, that question, that baffling sensation—none of it has ever left me. I've never been able to resolve it simply as my, or our, blessing. Often, I have thought God must be infuriated with me that I don't just see it that way. But for whatever reason, even being on the super-blessed and super-desired side of that scenario, something too human inside my spirit just refuses to let God off the hook about it. Though I can't fully sort it out, I'm guessing it's because I think if I had been one of the parents crying at that window, watching someone as insufficient as me walk off with a healthy baby, I would've spent as much or more time admonishing God as praying to Him.

Many years and a healthy son added to the mix later, I found myself sitting in the large atrium at the entrance of Toronto's globally renowned Hospital for Sick Children (SickKids). "[It is] recognized as one of the world's foremost paediatric health care institutions and is Canada's leading centre dedicated to advancing children's health through the integration of patient care, research and education." (From the website: www.sickkids.ca.)

SickKids is one of several of the greatest hospitals in the nation that are all located within the same few downtown Toronto city blocks. Thus, my work among the city's homeless population had me literally on their doorsteps time and time again over the years. My own children were fine and in school that day. The reason I was there was more about my own journey and my own unresolved business. Often I would walk inside SickKids and, well, the truth is I'm not even sure what I was doing there. I just used to sit there and watch people. Then talk to God lots. Mostly beg Him that if He were going to show up anywhere on any given day, He would choose *here.* As a dad, I just could not imagine anywhere more important for Him to show up. Inane prayers that completely undermined the Creator of the universe, but that were very sincere and representative of my meagre faith and its scope. The whole thing had ramped up in my soul enough that by that point, I had actually received permission from the executive director of Youth Unlimited to investigate a way for our agency to get involved with the hospital in some manner of comfort care. And this was one of the days I had awkwardly tried to knock on a few doors—figuratively and literally—to do so.

Ultimately, I found myself sitting alone in the foyer in the smallness of my limitations, just people watching and whispering to God once again. But I think that's where God likes to meet us most—in our smallness. I don't mean in defeat, or shame, or embarrassment. No God of love I would want anything to do with would want those things for us. I mean in a smallness that finds our hearts tender and meek. When I see and hear famous preachers and prominent evangelists on television, or in front of giant congregations, say they just received a word from God, I feel sick to my stomach. Not because it might not be true. I have strong doubts about it, for sure, but I guess it could be so. But mostly, I feel sick about the misleading notion that God likes to speak to us in our bigness, and that ultimately some people will then believe He will never speak to them. Surely God adores our smallness the same way a daddy does when he bundles up his toddler to play in the snow. Longing to stop time in the precious moments when innocence and dependence are in synch. Alive with anticipation, but small enough to need to be bundled up by the one who loves you.

Only minutes after I sat down, a young woman sat just to the left of me, several seats away. Far enough that I would not have been able to hear her if she spoke aloud, but close enough to see her clearly, and situated that passersby would not block her from my view. It's not that I was meaning to watch her, but the positioning made it impossible not to see her clearly anytime I simply looked ahead. If ever there was a place that I didn't need to leave a creepy impression, it was here.

Her eyes were red and puffy, having clearly just finished a good long cry. She fumbled through her bag and pulled out a drink box. She popped the straw in, took a sip, rested the juice on her lap, then drew her head back, facing the ceiling, and gave a long weepy sigh. She sat like that with her eyes closed for several seconds. I tried not to stare, but she was radiant in her quiet sorrow. But those seconds were only a brief reprieve, as she suddenly dropped her head and burst into tears again. If nothing else, she needed someone to bundle her up. And that's just what she got.

In came a little boy, four years old at most. He spotted her as soon as he entered the front doors and ran across the vestibule into her arms, with daddy only a few paces behind.

And her face. Oh, her face! That extraordinary face that only young adoring mommies can make happen. The one when a brave smile rises up in an attempt to deny tear-stained eyes and blotchy cheeks. The one reserved exclusively for their children in moments when mommies seek out the impossible courage to care for their beloved despite their own broken hearts. If you know the face I'm describing, then never again wonder if you have seen the face of God, for surely it is revealed in the face of every mommy in these moments.

CHAPTER 7

And mommy held the little boy tight, while daddy sat at her side and spoke softly in her ear. She kept her son pressed against her so he could not see the tears stream down her face while she and her husband whispered back and forth. While this was happening, the picture, as fully as I would ever be able to discern it, was becoming clearer. The little boy had run in waving a teddy bear with a pink ribbon around his neck for his mommy to see, and the daddy was carrying several items in a girl's flowery baby bag.

Finally, the little boy squeezed his way out of mommy's long embrace only to see her in the full flight of her anguish. His little jaw dropped when he looked over and saw that his daddy was not doing much better. As a child, there are few things—if any—more frightening than seeing your parents in a state of over-whelming distress.

I'm not sure what you're expecting to read next. That the mommy was able to find that brave mommy smile again? That the little boy joined in the crying, as much scared as sad? That the daddy pulled it together and did what we dad-dies always want to do and huddled everyone together, providing daring words of assurance? Good guesses. They would've been mine. But none of those things happened.

In fact, the mommy and daddy got worse. They fell into each other's arms and sobbed. But smallness prevailed. The little boy put the teddy bear between his knees, reached up, and stroked the sides of his mommy's and daddy's heads. I couldn't hear a word, but I could see him chatting away, rubbing his parents' cheeks as they wept. And he bundled them, and comforted them, not fully understanding everything and with no ability to change anything. But loving fully out of his smallness.

The nineteenth-century Bavarian-born writer Jean Paul Richter once said, "The smallest children are nearest to God, as the smallest planets are nearest the sun."

Indeed, small and near to God. There is nothing we should strive for more.

This backward wellspring of comfort went on for several glorious minutes, until a group of three nurses who were heading to the front doors stopped just before departing. One of them had taken notice of the little family in its strange and splendid huddle and sent her friends off so she could approach the little boy and his parents.

Lip reading and a dynamic too obvious to misread were now being captured by many others also sitting near and watching as covertly as possible. All of us watching this theatre of unanticipated sorrow and beauty play out.

The family all clearly recognized the sweet nurse as one of those who was tending to their baby girl. She kneeled beside the little boy and rubbed his back while he kept his tiny hands pressed against his parents' faces. She said nothing. She simply let whatever light she had to offer flow through the little boy. Then she stood, looked at the broken parents and pressed her crossed arms over her own breaking heart. She gently wiped her own cheeks and stepped away. Every movement was small and perfect.

But as she walked away, the little boy ran to catch her. She took a knee at his side and listened as he held the teddy bear up to her. His back was to me, making it impossible to do much more than guess at his little words, but her face was bright and alive as she listened and nodded back to him, an assurance to his request. She took the little bear with both hands without a moment's second-guessing. All of us watching read her lips clearly: "I promise."

Then the little boy threw his arms around her, gave her a tight squeeze, turned and ran back to his parents, knowing his gift would find its way to his baby sister.

By now there were a great many silent and misty-eyed spectators trying not to stare. Or at least not get caught. As the little boy returned to his mommy and daddy, I looked around me, shocked by how so many of us had unintentionally fallen hypnotically into the scene. But what was most remarkable at that point was that after the little boy returned to his family, everyone remained, watching the nurse as she stood alone in the distance with the little bear. She stood still, hugging the plush teddy as she watched the little boy rejoin his parents. The look on her face revealed a heart that knew only too well what it meant to bring hope gently, and receive hope quietly, and never question the exchange. She remained there a few seconds longer, then turned slowly and walked away.

Since the day my daughter was born, my soul has been continuously worn thin with the fear of having my children diagnosed with life-limiting illness or life-threatening conditions. The mommy and daddy I witnessed that day represent a trembling I cannot, and will not, ever find words for. And the brother to a tiny baby sister fighting for her life was, and is, the ultimate picture of inherent righteousness. So magnificently young and guided by angels to not spend a moment questioning what he could or could not do, but just loving fantastically.

And the nurse? Ah, the nurse. There was just something exceptional about the nurse. Only in sight for a minute. Two at the most. But there was something transcendent about her presence. Surely, she could've walked through the front doors for coffee with her pals, intentional about leaving the little family in their grief. Relished her break, guarded her lunch hour, fled after a long shift.

CHAPTER 7

Just taken her time, for her. How much giving does any one person need to do? How much grief does any one person need to bear? How much tenderness does any one person need to share before she can break for coffee, chatter with friends and experience a change of scenery? These were not the signs of a good employee loyal to a job description. These were not the hallmarks of a staffer who was able to complete tasks well. These were the unannounced, secretly heroic, prolific nuances of a hopegiver.

Of course, we all have the opportunity to be hopegivers. A four-year-old boy armed with nothing more than a teddy bear and heavenly instinct is more than enough proof of that. But there is another classification of hopegivers that our busy society has found easy to take for granted, if not forget.

Nurses don't enter the nursing field to clean bedpans and tolerate shift work. No one steps into a career serving people with intellectual disabilities because wiping drool and tempering seizures pays well. I have never known anyone working in a shelter who aspired to clean urine-stained bedsheets or break up fights. And no child ever played schoolteacher and imagined being threatened by students or parents, or navigating a complex infrastructure that often feels like it's working against you. None entered as task-doers. At the core, somewhere in the early stages, they all entered as hopegivers. Ready to take on the associated tasks, prepared to tend to the related details and educated for the cause, yes. But ultimately spirited and fuelled by the one thing that cannot be measured by scale or salary. The heart of a hopegiver. Where promises are not made, but prayers are a promise. Where justice is not denied, but mercy refuses second place. Where power is not a pursuit, but compassion is counted as nothing less than your greatest strength. And where an imagination for celebrating against the odds thrives.

During a routine ultrasound early in her pregnancy, my dear friend, Annie, along with her husband, Paul, were surprised by the announcement that heart abnormalities were identified. The prognosis worsened in short order, and they were told that life itself was highly improbable for their son, and even with extensive surgical intervention after birth, a meagre percent diagnosed as such live beyond the toddler years.

I'm not sure I have ever known people to cling to their faith or believe for miracles the way Annie and Paul have. And in that, from the first of their many consistent and detailed updates sent to friends and family, they have faithfully called on people to stand with them as hopegivers. And even as I write this, and as their six-month-old baby boy, Miles, defies the odds and soldiers his way through surgeries and procedures, Annie and Paul honour the hopegivers as vital: "We needed support. We needed people who would stand with us in the face of those odds and believe—no, fight—for a miracle."

Among all of Annie and Paul's liturgical updates and awe-inspiring testimonials, there has been one thing that has been a continual spark in their story for me—the professionals who have shown up in their roles as hopegivers, identified in passages such as these:

"We met Gwyneth that night, and it just felt like a gift...a perfect God appointment for us. We felt comfortable with her right away and knew she was the right person to walk through this with us" (28th week of pregnancy).

"We had an ultrasound with a great nurse who showed us that Miles is very much head down, and is in a position they call 'occiput anterior,' which is ideal for labour. She also told us that my body is doing an awesome job of growing a healthy-sized baby boy" (33rd week of pregnancy).

"We figure what she saw was the fruit of the 'progressive healing miracle' that God's been doing in Miles' heart" (Days before Miles' birth).

"This was such a gift to us. We praise God for sending us Rebecca to watch over Miles in those first few days" (The week after Miles was born).

"That was a gift that Liz helped give me...Not only did she care for Miles in such a professional and caring way, but she cared for us and supported us in ways I can only begin to explain" (From an unsolicited letter of commendation and thanksgiving sent to SickKids five months after Miles' birth).

To bring hope to the hopegivers. To recognize them, identify them and esteem them. To serve them as they serve others. To celebrate them. Essential! But too seldom, if at all, does it occur. Perhaps it is that absence that keeps things from really changing in the world. The scarcity that steals enthusiasm, allows fatigue to conquer, and ultimately sanctions hierarchies to be built on competitiveness, rather than the formation of community.

In an episode that took less than five minutes, I was to bear witness with a group of unidentified strangers to what the gentle splendour of a true hope exchange looks like, feels like, and is. From every angle, love and compassion were extended in extravagance: mom to son, husband to wife, son to parents, nurse to little boy, little boy to nurse. And why? Over a baby girl who was not even in their midst, but was in the centre of their hearts.

Like everything that is truly good, a hope exchange is not to be squandered. The opportunities to speak life into one another are moments tantamount to knowing brilliance "on earth as it is in heaven" (Matthew 6:10, NIV). And even if language fails and phrases falter, there are urgent and unscripted silent moments that speak these matters best. Ideally, we would all know what those moments look and feel like. I am positive this is the heart of God.

But in case you're uncertain, find a nurse who's been hugged by a small child with thanksgiving, and ask. I'm sure that she, or he, can tell you. If not with words, just by the look on their face.

Father, Don't Take This Life

(lyrics written in the lobby of The Hospital for Sick Children; Copyright, T.J. Huff, 2001)

As simply as I can, as broken as I am,
When You find me in the dark—can we make a deal, God?
We're almost out of time, so God, will You read my mind?
And forgive me when I pray, and I say:
Father, don't take this life.
God, not today. Father, it can't be right.
How else can I pray?

Waiting in the cold, with nothing left to hold on to.
When the breathing ends, will the silence be my friend?
Time is out of reach, and my final plea is peace.

Forgive me, God, today when I pray:
Father, don't take this life.
God, not today. Father, it can't be right.
How else can I pray?

This road has been so long. How will we go on?
How will we find our way?
There is no pain like this; this final kiss
Before angels make their way.

And when the struggle's done, and your angels finally come,
Sail, "my love," I pray, in a river of light, God.
May heaven's skies be warm, as "our love" is reborn
And teach us God today, to pray:

Father, to make this right.
God, all this pain.
Father, we need Your light.
I will never be the same.

This road has been so long. How will we go on?
How will we find our way?
There is no pain like this; this final kiss
Before angels make their way.

The Sound of Music was Rodgers and Hammerstein's final musical collaboration. Based on the memoirs of Maria von Trapp, the Broadway production found its way to the silver screen, and ultimately to unimaginable favour as one of the most beloved films of all time. Revivals of the stage production continue to delight audiences around the world.

The Sound of Music is the first movie I ever saw in a movie theatre. While it was originally released in 1965, it was during a re-release some five years later that included smaller towns and cities when I was first and completely awed by it as a little boy. My family didn't have expendable means for treats such as sit-down restaurants or overnight hotel stays, so anything such as a trip to a movie theatre was both a huge adventure and an extraordinary luxury.

We drove from my grandfather's rustic home along the shores of Lake Huron to the small city of Owen Sound. While we were from the large metropolis of Toronto, to anyone in my grandfather's region Owen Sound was considered the big city. Originally inhabited by the Ojibway people, it became a rowdy seaport, known among sailors as "Little Liverpool." The day-long anticipation of going into Owen Sound to see a real movie was incredible. Entering the dimly lit theatre holding my mom's hand and sitting in the big plush red seats felt like make-believe. And the movie itself was spellbinding for a little boy who had never seen or heard anything like it. To this very day, not one second of that memory is lost on me.

"I go to the hills when my heart is lonely, I know I will hear what I've heard before, My heart will be blessed with the sound of music, And I'll sing once more."

These are the glorious last four lines of lyrics in the sweeping title track. Though I was far too young to comprehend the gravity of liberation by way of music, even then I knew that, whatever the words meant, and the way they rode the melody, all of this would one day catch up to me.

From years of piano lessons throughout childhood to bit parts in elementary school musicals—from the little boy lead as slingshot Bible hero David in a church cantata to dreaming of rock fortune on the drums at age 14 in a sloppy cottage band—my childhood musical aspirations were marred by average-at-best ability, nerves and impatience.

Ultimately, if not astonishingly, it was the deaf community that inspired me to dig deeper for the truest treasure of music, and to find my place in it.

My wife, Diane, is the child of two deaf parents. Both Keith and Jane were born profoundly deaf due to viral infections their mothers processed during their first trimesters of pregnancy—rubella and chicken pox, neither of which causes hereditary deafness. As a child, living with her family in a Milwaukee suburb in the early 1940s, Jane was often left on the outside of common little girl hijinks and play. A fiercely protective older brother took care of anyone who would dare tease, in no uncertain terms. But that would not replace the void left by not fitting in and being left out.

While they seemingly had nothing in common but age and proximity, there was another little boy in Jane's neighbourhood who found himself on the outside looking in too. A little boy named Walter. A boy whose best friend was not a person, but rather an inanimate object. The piano.

Consigned to his father's taskmaster demands, Walter was permitted no opportunity to roughhouse or play sports with the other boys in the community. All of Walter's time outside school was relegated to the difficult memory work and mastering of technique required to become a marvellous pianist.

Day after day, as she passed by, Jane would notice Walter through an open window, sitting alone at the piano. And Walter would notice Jane walking down the sidewalk all alone. One day, Walter motioned Jane to the front door and invited her in. And there, among the unlikeliest of friends, in the unlikeliest of places, music served the soul and allowed for a sanctuary of belonging. A childhood kinship blossomed as little deaf Jane pressed her small hands against the sides of the piano while Walter played Beethoven and Brahms.

Wladziu Valentino, a.k.a. Walter, a.k.a. Lee, went on to the highest heights of fame and fortune imaginable, known around the world simply by his last name. Liberace. The highest-paid entertainer in the world, even as Elvis Presley and the Beatles were at their heights of popularity. But long before the flamboyance and larger-than-life persona he created, long before the schmaltz and glitz that overpowered his remarkable genius, and long before radio and television brought him into millions of living rooms—he was just a little boy in his own living room, finding friendship with a little deaf girl by way of music.

The mysterious power of music overcoming its most formidable opponent—deafness—is a story endemic with tales of unexpected celebration. Ludwig von Beethoven's being among the most infamous. One of the most influential and celebrated composers in all of history, Beethoven suffered from a severe form of tinnitus that worsened as he aged. By the time the 1824 Vienna premiere for his Symphony No. 9 in D Minor ("Ode to Joy") was upon him, lesions on a "distended inner ear" had led to profound deafness. Historical accounts tell that Beethoven stood at the front of the stage, near to the conductor Michael Umlauf, with his own baton and score in a frenetic attempt to share in the direction from his post. At the conclusion of the performance, Umlauf walked over to Beethoven and turned him to face the audience so that he would see what he could not hear; a packed house on its feet in jubilant applause that continued for an unprecedented five repeat standing ovations. The sound of music lost on his ears. But only his ears.

I didn't know Beethoven's story, Diane's mom's story, or much—if anything—about how truly transcendent God's gift of music is when I first arrived at the Ontario Camp of the Deaf at age 16. While I was unprepared for what was to come, I learned quickly to make no assumptions about deafness or the deaf community from the moment I arrived. The first thirty minutes of the first evening program that gathered everyone together was spent singing. When my friend Derek, whose family founded and led the camp, stood up front and said (and signed), "Okay, let's sing," I was in shock. In fact, I thought he was joking and wondered if the deaf would be offended. But one by one, deaf children eagerly and enthusiastically volunteered to stand at his side and lead the others in song.

There were few, if any, contemporary songs. Most of what was standard fare at deaf camp were traditional Sunday school songs taught and re-taught by the old and faithful generation of deaf adults sustaining the deaf church. But for my entire 15-summer tenure at the camp, no matter what new songs were introduced, no matter how wild or rag-tagged the camper population was, they loved singing the old church basement staples.

I'm not sure what hit me first—the sight or the sound. I always sat at the back of whichever room we were gathered in, my first summer at the camp, for two reasons. One—to spare myself as much embarrassment as possible, never able to keep up. Two—because from that vantage point I could see everything, including the ridiculous beauty of all those hands moving in unison.

Chapter 8

If that weren't enough, there was an indescribable splendour to the sound of it all. In the few seconds between when Derek said, "Let's sing" and when we actually did, I thought to myself—*Well, this will be interesting. The room will be silent.*

Not even close. It was the loudest unamplified singing I had ever heard. Some of the hard-of-hearing kids near the front found a bit of Derek's range to follow. But for the most part, it was a wonderfully uninhibited opportunity for everyone to create the sounds as they were able, as they guessed they should be, and as they had projected them all their lives. Made even more vivacious and opportunistic by being in the presence of your peers, in a place of absolute belonging.

Scientifically, it's believed that sign language operates out of the same brain departments as spoken language. This would at least begin to shed light on the incredible dexterity and communicative abilities of deaf toddlers and preschoolers who often exceed the communication skills of hearing children their own age. And one of the most intriguing assertions made in context to profoundly deaf people—deaf from birth—is that they possess an auditory inner voice, separate from the one that allows a person to wonder, ponder or day-dream. Just as we all do, but that theirs is created independently around lan-guage as they suppose it, have read or learned it, and have watched it (such as by lip reading). The discussion is as fascinating as it is mind-boggling.

By the time I had made my way to the camp, the rock band that Derek and I were playing in was just beginning to take itself seriously. Our originals were on par with what goofy teenagers come up with in their garages, our sound and abilities were nothing unique, but our commitment and enthusiasm were over the top. And our training ground was impossible to imitate.

Outside our faithful base of encouraging friends, we found our first legs in a world that could only be considered no less than Spinal Tap-esque. Our ear-liest and most faithful fans were deaf children, teenagers, adults and even senior citizens. While we sold or gave away a few tapes to hard-of-hearing kids who would listen to them through walkmans at full volume, we had countless deaf youth and adults sporting T-shirts bearing our logo.

By my third summer at the camp, our bass player, Steve, had joined the camp staff as well, as a lifeguard. Three-quarters of the band Double Edge were already on-site. So, our drummer Al—the only guy with a "real" summer job—would then drive up every Friday afternoon, and we would have two or three standing gigs every weekend. We were playing more summertime gigs as a house band for deaf kids than most professionals were doing on the road for the hearing. We'd play in the main hall with carpet-covered wood floors, and turn the main speakers face down so the rattle and hum was bombastic from the ground up. We'd play in the gym for deaf dance nights with every volume knob cranked to ten. We let developmentally and physically challenged kids lean against the drums and sit on the amps as though on theme park rides. We let hard-of-hearing kids scream into the mics and get euphoric hearing their own voices come back to them through the floor monitors. And when all the campers were down for the night, we Pied-Pipered every off-duty staff person with any inclination to join us—deaf or hearing—to a nearby abandoned maple sugar shack that we had commandeered, and jammed into the wee hours. And always with someone up front, standing in with the band, interpreting every lyric of every song.

These were strange and wonderful days indeed. Impossible for anyone to duplicate in the contemporary age of political correctness, protocol and organizational discipline. But what we lacked in discernment, we gained in a truly shared sense of adventure. What we bypassed in convention, we made up for in memories. We learned the meaning of a good lyric, as signed words never fell victim to a bad PA—and there was always someone who'd ask what those words meant. We learned to keep the beat steady by watching deaf dancers more faithful to the time signature than we were. And we were humbled by some of the grandest guest lead singers of all time as Down syndrome kids took to the mic and repeatedly stole the show. The absolute truth is that we were only ready for the hearing after we'd been honed by the deaf. By far, these were some of the happiest moments of my entire life.

But while it was indeed among the deaf, the moment I first experienced music's capacity to transcend my own sensibility had nothing to do with science, volume or escapade. It came during my very first summer at the camp, when I couldn't get myself out of something I wanted dearly to be out of.

The camp's morning routine was old school. Small groups of campers, defined by age, rotated between three sessions: swimming and waterfront activities, arts and crafts, and values-focused Bible lessons. The camper response was as old school as the routine, proving that kids are kids, deaf or hearing. Predictably, the waterfront always the favourite, the craft room a not-too-distant second, and the sit-down Bible class always trailing far, far behind.

In my early days at the camp, things were as much all-hands-on-deck as they were task or position oriented. So it was not absurd to find yourself leaping off cliffs in the morning, dressed like a clown for lunch, peeling potatoes in the late afternoon and spying for cabin escapees at night. While for most activities and deeds there were few options but to jump in and learn fast, I was generally out of harm's way when it came to even being considered to lead Bible classes. And as far as I was concerned, this was the one upside to my limited signing abilities.

But residential summer camps are bubbles. Each one bears its own distinct societal landscape, with norms, demands and opportunities that would seem implausible outside the bubble. And one of the norms is that whatever is needed, and whatever has to happen to get things done, will surely be planned for the bubble from within the bubble. At no time is that more evident than when sickness runs through a weary camp staff. Which, by way of equal parts responsibility and frolic, is completely inevitable.

And so, on a hot summer day in the region of the breathtaking Muskokas, just days before my 17th birthday, when all the Bible class top dogs were down for the count, after one back-up possibility gave way to the next, which gave way to the next, I was left alone in the sunny corner of a camp chapel with five deaf children between the ages of four and six. I was terrified.

The children were extraordinary. They sat cross-legged in front of me and yip-yapped amongst themselves with lightning fast tiny fingers. And I let them. As far as I was concerned, an internally self-structured peer discussion group was anything but too lofty for this assembly of kindergarteners. But eventually they caught on. I wasn't waiting on them—I was hiding from them. Finally, one little boy looked at me, leaned forward, shrugged his little shoulders and grunted, as if to say—"Well, do something." So I did.

The only reason I could afford to work those early years at a summer camp was because I made money through the school year drawing comic strips for community newspapers and magazines. So, trapped in the moment, I counted on the only thing I knew. If a picture was worth a thousand words, and I only knew how to sign about fifty—well, a picture it would be. So for 40 minutes I drew picture after picture of every single creature I could think of that might have floated on, flown by or swam beneath Noah's ark, until eventually, with 15 gruelling minutes to go, the only marker I had ran out of ink.

With nothing left in my sad arsenal, I finally went to the one place I knew they'd be glad to go.

"Let's sing."

This 15 minutes ultimately changed the course of my entire life.

Without any mortal leading, guiding or coaxing, five wee children absent of frequency and amplitude led their own way through the magnificence of song and the enormity of heaven. Gleefully pacing themselves through the assurances of "Jesus Loves Me" and "Jesus Loves the Little Children," without distraction or doubt. Exchanging the sound of music for the sight of music, and celebrating it with no less delight. Small buzzing voices whispered and chirped, harmonizing to the incomprehensible melody of miniature hands. It was a world unto itself. One I had never known. One I had never imagined. One I longed to be a part of.

To offer up what we do have rather than hide behind what we don't, to find and share joy in the abandonment of self-consciousness, to hear music with our hearts and uncover our own unique and uninhibited way to song, and to seek joy with the hearts of children—surely these are the signposts to God's Kingdom.

"I tell you the truth, unless you change and become like little children, you will never enter the kingdom of heaven" (Matthew 18:3, NIV).

I continued through my teenage and college years, young adulthood, through parenthood, and into my I-should-know-better-by-now years making countless foolish mistakes and taking endless blessings for granted. But I have never heard children's Sunday school songs the same way since that day. And, were it not for a few tiny deaf children, I know I would have never fully known what music really is.

What else can we long to be but boundless in imagining that God can make music through anyone, and for everyone?

It was the final game of a select-level hockey tournament, and my goal-tender son was anxious heading into it, not wanting to let the team down. Eager to be sharp, fully attentive, and at his very best, Jake had been playing out the game in his head since the moment he knew he was getting the call to go between the pipes. I'm not sure what the pressure of being a team's goalie feels like, but I sure know the ridiculous misplaced stress of being a net-minder's parent. I stood outside the door of my 12-year-old son's team dressing room and listened intently as the coach implored the kids to "leave it all on the ice."

Hearing the words through the door rattled me. Not because they were bad or uncommon. Just because of what they meant. Along with comedic math assurances of someone having somehow given more than 100 per cent of themselves, these are the routine words that gold medal Olympians and multimillion dollar sports heroes drop religiously after event-driven successes:

I left it all on the ice. I left it all on the field. I left it all on the court. I left it all...

As parents, my wife and I have encouraged our children at every turn, and in all things, to do their very best and try their hardest. They have always known that the marks on their school report cards don't mean half as much to us as the teacher's comments about effort and character. And we have stayed the course in teaching that giving your best honours God and others, and shows appreciation for opportunities and blessings like nothing else. But be it swimming lessons, music lessons, team or individual sports, class projects or whatever, I had never asked my daughter or son to "leave it all" anywhere. And until that day, I had never heard anyone else ask that of them either.

I had a few inconspicuous mid-life crisis moments that day, standing outside that arena dressing room. They started while contemplating that my little boy was already man enough to carry the weight of such words. Those emotions were heightened, recognizing that my daughter had long since passed the stage of having to know the gravity of such endless grown-up pressures and stresses. And as the team door swung open and my son's team poured onto the rink, I wondered if I had done everything I could to prepare him. Not simply for the game that day, or those yet to come, but for a world that thrives on heroes and scapegoats. For a world that isn't afraid to define people by singular moments. For a world that is glad to announce whether any one person's "leaving it all" was—or is—enough.

Jake made the saves, "left it all on the ice," and his team won the tournament. His loving mom and adoring sister were at their teary-eyed best. His grandma and grandpa were elated. And his dad was too proud to speak. But not because his team had won. I had seen Jake win in heart-stoppers and lose in heartbreakers many times before. But because the little boy still in my mind's eye was, in fact, becoming a young man brave enough to take on challenges where I could not intervene.

Minor hockey goaltenders are always among the last to leave the dressing room after a game. Other players, sans the extra gear to change out of, depart with their parents in comparatively short order, and thus there are always a few minutes for goalie parents to wait in relative silence. I found myself standing outside the dressing room doors, all alone, in the exact same spot where I had had an epiphany just over an hour earlier, pondering—who had I seen or known who'd, so-to-speak, "left it all" anywhere?

Well, you don't spend much time enduring—or occasionally even enjoying—Sunday school for years on end and miss out on the obvious "right" answers to that question. For us pre-high-tech era children—flannelgraph Bible stories, hand-motion songs, and white bread colouring books never missed a beat in spelling that one out pretty clearly. But I hadn't actually seen those saints with my own two eyes, and, in these human moments, I wasn't really thinking in terms of a sacrificial "Saviour." Those thoughts came quick and first, but lasted mere moments. Far too apparent and transcendent. I was still in the brain space of sportscasts, comic books and rock music—much easier, if not effortless, mental traffic to play in.

However, as I did play it out in my mind, surprisingly, touchdown and home run heroes didn't come to mind either. Neither did caped crusaders or pop superstars. Of all things, what came to mind were two old men. Both of whom I became aware of at the same time, when I was a wee boy. And, as far as I knew, they had nothing in common outside age and my admiration. One was on my black and white television set. The other, outside my front door. For me, one will always be the epitome of "leaving it all" professionally. But it was while thinking of him that my mind drew near to the memories of the other—who taught me, without even knowing it, that *where* we have the opportunities to "leave it all," give it all, and be at our best is not the measure of someone's character. Only that we do. For the famed few, that may be on Broadway stages, movie screens and fields of glory. For others, it will be recognized by way of academic degrees, service awards and medals of honour. Some will be toasted, roasted and eulogized. But perhaps the greatest of all testimonials will never leave the front porch.

I recall as a little boy, around the age of five or six—the same age my son first started playing hockey—watching the unique Red Skelton on television, with my parents. I didn't fully understand everything he said or did, but I was keenly aware of the fact that every character he played out—no matter how dishevelled or peculiar—made people smile, laugh and feel good.

The son of a circus clown, Red Skelton had a celebrated career that began with paying his dues in burlesque and vaudeville in the late 1920s and moved successfully and sequentially into radio, movies and television. Nearing the end of his illustrious career and long life, Red Skelton would tour across North America as a one-man comedy and musical stage show. During those remarkable late 1980s and early 1990s live stage shows, I often had the unique opportunity to watch Red's work from the side of the stage, standing next to his personal assistants and stagehands. Likewise to visit and chat briefly with him in his dressing room.

Red was committed to making everyone laugh, making everyone smile and making everyone feel connected. This included those who couldn't hear. Thus, he insisted on hiring an interpreter for the deaf to have on stage for every show. My young wife, Diane, a sign language interpreter at the time, was his repeat on-stage interpreter for the Toronto and Ottawa shows when his tour brought him through Canada. Quite often, in fact, she even had small roles to play in some of Red's performance jokes. This afforded me one of the rarest opportunities of my life, to bear witness to a comedic legend and movie star from behind the scenes and get a glimpse of the soul beneath the performer when the curtain was down. A journeyman's soul that somehow afforded Red Skelton, among other things, a unique understanding of the hobo life and how it crosses over with the life of a sad clown. It was captured in his words, songs, mimes, sketches and his now infamous paintings.

The man himself, his wide array of skills and these rare opportunities were terribly interesting for me. I knew that my parents and their friends of the same generation were extremely intrigued by our opportunities to meet him up close. I was keenly aware of the reverence held for such radio and television icons from the media pioneering era. Plus, I had witnessed his impact as someone very special who made everyone laugh while on our family TV so many years ago. And so, for me, first and foremost, he was simply a big star.

But it was his way, when watching him up close, that would always surprise me. Backstage, I would often join Diane when she was called to his dressing room to discuss the show and be paid. Even business with Red was "old school." His road manager, producer and handlers never paid Diane for her work. And there was no paper trail or contract to sign. Red would hunt around his dressing room for his wallet, checking his tuxedo jacket on the door, his overcoat on the chair, and on and on until he found it. Then he would reach in and pull out whatever amount was in it, and that was what she got paid. Sometimes two hundred dollars. Sometimes four or even five hundred dollars. No rhyme or reason, or any kind of scale. Just whatever he was carrying. Which—while we were young and still paying off our college loans—always felt like a huge windfall.

And still, if all these factors weren't enough, having myself just entered the fray of work among homeless people, it was his take on hoboism that compelled and surprised me most.

In 1951, when CBS brought his radio show to television, Red introduced what was then his newest character, a "hobo" named Freddy the Freeloader. As the world has changed, so has its enormous sensitivities, and its accompanying language. Some for the better, some for the worse. But every nuance of Mr. Skelton's tender work makes it easy for me to believe that if he could, in and for this day and age, he would change Freddie's moniker to something less politically incorrect or stigmatizing than "the Freeloader." Perhaps just "Freddie the Free."

Red Skelton had a famous introduction for Freddie. As he sat in front of a dressing room mirror placed on stage and applied sad clown makeup while transitioning into character, he began his gentle soliloquy this way:

"Freddie the Freeloader is a little bit of you, and a little bit of me. A little bit of all of us, y'know?"

He went on to share a bit about Freddy's simple and pure understanding of love and time, respect and honour. And he would close with this:

"He's nice to everybody, because he was taught that man was made in God's image. He's never met God in person, and the next fellow just might be Him. I would say Freddy is a little bit of all of us."

I remember standing in the wings of one of Toronto's great theatre stages, watching and listening to this for the first time, guessing I might be the only person in the great venue who needed to accept those words—not just for my heart, but for my very vocation. I thought to myself—*Really? C'mon, I mean, really? God is trying to talk to me through Red Skelton?*

More than enough fodder for a good tale, none of these matters compares to the last time I saw Red Skelton at work. He closed all his Canadian shows the same way, sharing an inspiring ode he had written about the nation of Canada, while the orchestra played the national anthem below his words in a constant crescendo to the speech's (and show's) climactic closing moment. It was melodramatic and authentic, calculated and beautiful, all at once. And it never failed. Every night, it sealed the deal on the promise of departing to a standing ovation.

While the routine never changed over the years I witnessed it, the health and endurance of the legend did. From stage left, behind the curtain, I saw what only his closest keepers knew. The true cost of his performance, and the toll of his commitment.

The curtain was always set to close for just a few seconds at the end of his lengthy performance, just long enough for people to rise to their feet. Then it would open and allow him one last bow to his adoring fans as a finale. Not long enough for stagehands and assistants to reach him. There was a surreal ten seconds between when the curtain would close and re-open, and the aged icon stood alone in the dark. I will never forget the sight of his silhouette changing once the final crack of light was shut out by the closed curtain. His stature dropped a good six to eight inches as he wobbled in the dark to keep his balance. But then, like a marionette, as soon as that curtain opened for one more round of blowing kisses to the audience, he became the larger-than-life star he knew people expected him to be.

Then he stepped back from the stage lights one last time, and as the curtain literally fell for the last time, Red's people scooted along behind it to catch him. Two men from each side, one steering a wheelchair. Slumped into the chair, he was wheeled off in an instant, flanked by his protectors, all while the crowd cheered on in hope of one more curtain call.

Red Skelton knew his craft, adored those who adored him, meant to make his mark by bringing joy, and most of all, he knew—long, long, long past the time he needed to prove himself—what it meant to "leave it all" on the stage, while staying true to his quote:

"I personally believe that each of us was put here for a purpose—to build, not to destroy. If I can make people smile, then I have served my purpose for God."

But it's not always simple to absorb the things that inspire us, drive us, or motivate us most. It is much easier to focus on a successful end result (like an adoring crowd) and assume what got you there was good and right. But can anyone ever really take the stage without being driven in some way by ego and pride? Play sports competitively? Be a leader? Preach a sermon? Or, hmm, write a book?

My parents modelled "leaving it all" in countless sacrifices of struggle and blue-collar hard work, while never cutting short what it meant to serve the community, church, family or friends. They had to thrive on the kind of pride that comes from putting in a good day's work, making leftovers last, and never assuming anything. Their names have never been in lights and no one has ever asked for their autographs. But what they taught me by doing what they had to do, and doing the little things they could do, shaped me beyond compare.

My father worked at de Havilland Aircraft for 25 years, helping build planes for happy vacationers, before he ever had the opportunity to take a commercial flight himself. In fact, my parents' own little romantic ritual away from my brothers and I was to take a thermos of tea or a bottle of Pepsi and two plastic cups, go for a ride to the west end of the city, sit outside the airport runways and watch the planes come and go to places they could only dream of. I learned at a very young age to enjoy what you can, rather than be bitter about what you can't. But, even still, it was never simple to have friends whose parents did have the resources for airplane trips to sunny destinations, Friday night restaurants and enrolling their kids in organized sports leagues. One of the greatest childhood sadnesses for me was that I never got to play in a hockey league, like my son does. Still, and so, adventure, play, fun and nearly every happy childhood memory I have came from experiences that cost zero dollars and zero cents.

And that is where the other old man comes in.

Schofie.

His full name was Theodore (Ted) Schofield, but I didn't know that until I was much older. He was born in 1900. As my mom tells it, at age five I just walked through the front door one day, shortly after we'd moved into the house we would live in for the rest of my childhood and teenage years, and said, "I made a new friend. His name is Schofie." Too little to take on "Mister Schofield," this nickname stuck, and soon was used by my family and the entire neighbourhood.

Schofie lived in a semi-detached house kitty-corner to my home. From our little front porch you could clearly see him seated on his. As far as I could tell as a little boy, he didn't do much more than sit on an old rusty kitchen chair that he left on his rickety porch and smoke cigarettes all day. In fact, that's both my first memory of him as a small child and my last memory of him as a young adult.

But one day, I was kicking a pop can around on my driveway and it bounced onto the road. The end of our driveway met with a very tight bend in the road that left a harsh blind spot for oncoming drivers, so I had clear instructions that I was never to step onto the road when on my own. Still, my childhood was spent calculating which was of greater value—complete obedience or not getting caught. As I would often do, I deemed the misdemeanour relatively harmless and reasonably likely to go unnoticed. I ventured out after my makeshift soccer ball, picked it up, and was ready to race back before my mom peeked out the front door when a crackly voice called to me from the other side. I took the risk, more intrigued by the old man than the consequences. After brief introductions, he left me standing still on the sidewalk, waiting for him to retrieve something he told me he'd found. He shuffled to his porch stairs, reached down behind a shrub and pulled out a large orange sponge ball. It was the size of a normal soccer ball, but made entirely of tightly packed sponge with no covering on it, and a giant chunk of it missing as though a dog had been at it. But indeed, it was better than my ginger ale can. Schofie and I would go on to play catch with that same old beaten-up ball on his tiny front lawn for many summers to follow.

I had a number of great and rambunctious friends as a child. We jumped makeshift ramps on our bikes, caught critters in the Humber River, climbed trees to our peril, crushed pennies on the railway tracks, and did anything and everything we could find to do that cost nothing more than time and interest, and the willingness to accept a dare. But without a doubt, as I play it back in my mind, as unlikely as it was, my best friend as a child was a very scruffy, unkempt old man with yellow cigarette-stained fingers who seldom ventured further than his own ten-foot-square front lawn.

In fact, I have a treasured picture of my seventh birthday party in our back-yard with Schofie at my side. My mom would always make a cake from scratch for birthdays, and we would have a backyard picnic for mine because it was in August. We could not afford anything elaborate or to have many friends over. But Schofie was always there.

I was never allowed to go into his home. And I never did. This was one agreement made with my parents that was not negotiable or sneak-worthy. Schofie's past was a complete mystery to me, and only portions were known to my parents, with more and more revealed over time by his own candour, the occasional visiting mystery relative, and a few neighbourhood facts and rumours. But I never griped, cared or asked for more leeway or information, because somehow he made that creaky old front porch more than enough safe fun and magic for me.

CHAPTER 9

For years, whenever I stepped out the front door, more often than not I would hear, "Timmy! Timmy!" and see Schofie waving me over for a few minutes of storytelling or to give me one of the little animal figures he had made out of candy wrappers. I don't have one single memory of being frightened, worried, harmed or anything other than blessed and thankful.

And that in itself is truly uncommon. To find a heart-rendering and published story of a small child and a mysterious old man that doesn't ultimately reveal an awkward twist, creepy outcome or painful experience. What a shameful reality that is. And while my parents' watchful eyes deserve much credit, I don't believe that's why my story is different. Likewise, though my family and some other very sweet families took more and more interest in Schofie and in helping him get by as he got older—thus him becoming more and more familiar to the wider neighbourhood—I don't believe that's why either.

Whatever Schofie had lived, lost, suffered or damaged in his life, by the time five-year-old Timmy showed up, he had learned to do what many people never do: to live and give in the moment. Regardless of the painful past.

It was only long after Schofie's death that I heard of, or came to know of, some of the woes of his life story. Why by age 70 he spent so much time all alone on his front porch. Why he couldn't at least afford a nice chair on a painted porch. Why the kind families on the street would be the ones required to assist feeding and cleaning him in his final lonely years. But despite all the "whys," as far as I'm concerned, the end result was this.

Schofie entered the wintertime of his life knowing well what it meant to say, "I left it all." Not in an arena or on a playing field, absorbing the ruckus of cheering fans. Not on stage, holding out and hanging in for the final curtain call and the applause of adoring fans. And maybe not soon enough, or good enough, for a great many that knew him in his younger years. But even still, before it was all over, he left it all on the front porch for a little boy who loved having a friend who was funny, safe, humble, interesting and interested. A gifting not lost by time, but rather one more appreciated and impactful as time goes on.

Whatever regrets Schofie had when his life ended, he surely had one less than I have now. Because as I grew from a little boy to a young man, inevitably I found less and less time for Schofie. He still called, "Timmy! Timmy!" when he saw me, but by the time girls and a driver's license were part of my life, I would whisk past Schofie so quickly as I came and went that I didn't have much more than a wave to offer. I wonder how many times he wished I still wanted to bounce the ball with him or catch beetles in a jar and name them. I would give anything to turn back time and fix that. I can barely write the words without feeling a pain in my chest.

The truth is, Schofie and I had so very little in common. His life was ending and mine was just beginning. His body was weakening every day as mine grew stronger. His head was filled with memories I was unaware of, and mine was filled with an imagination for things he would never know. But God's got to have a better handle on His beloved than to have everything make sense in my feeble mind and fit together by my agenda. Yikes. If not, I'd ultimately find everything hopeless, useless or opportunistic. He doesn't line up our relationships from shortest to tallest, in alphabetical order, by colour swatches or computer codes. Yet somehow, absurdly, we can, like to, and in fact do that ourselves.

I think He simply sets us in motion, longing for us to do that right thing in His name. To leave it all when and where it matters most. And to not take a single moment for granted.

The very month I began writing this chapter, my son won the award for outstanding goalie in his division. He left it all on the ice. And I cheered. Ironically, a week later I caught an old classic Red Skelton movie airing on cable. He left it all on the stage. And I laughed. And today, while looking for inspired final words to complete this chapter, I drove to the street I grew up on and stood in front of the porch where Schofie and I talked, laughed and played. He left it all on his porch. And I cried.

But words to share with you did not come so much as words I was to receive.

"Timmy! Timmy!"

Who will remember you saying their name with such affection and thanksgiving? And what could matter more? There is no greater way to celebrate someone.

And the price tag? Zero dollars and zero cents.

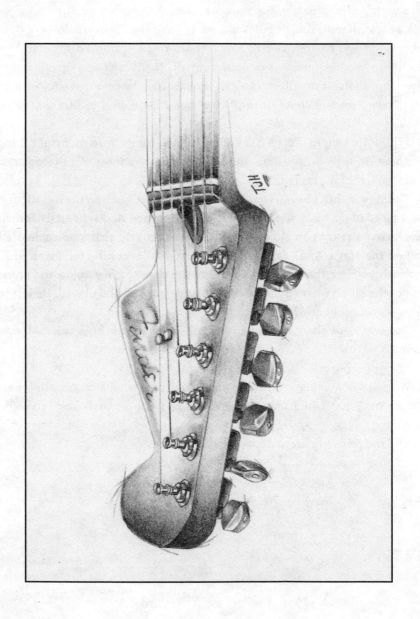

I suppose it's true that there's a line drawn in the sand for everything. Some days, I'm glad that's true. Some days, I'm not. But mostly I just wish I knew where it was.

Matters of the heart. Matters of integrity. Matters of honour. Matters of advocacy. Matters of self-defence. Matters of victory. Matters of denial. Matters of privacy. Matters of matters I don't even want to think about, but that matter most of all. Sigh. It seems every matter has a line drawn in the sand that is not meant to be crossed.

Indeed, life would be much simpler if at least these lines were considered universal. If they didn't change based on an endless number of ever-changing variables. A list of inconsistencies skewed by the greatest caveat of all—the human condition.

You'd think that the combination of accessibility to Holy Scripture, mind-bending studies of the laws of physics, consistent evidence of shocking human frailty, and endless episodes of Sesame Street would do the trick. That for the most part we would know what's up, what's best and what's what. But somehow, civilization after civilization has had its collective heart broken and mind numbed, ultimately resorting to the same futile resolve.

Guesswork.

At no other time in my life did I depend on guesswork the way I did in my late teens and early twenties. I guessed my way through the final year of high school, a year of art college, and two successful years of community college by fast-talking the slow-talking teachers, slow-talking the fast-talking teachers, and never missing free marks for attendance. Ultimately, I entered full-time youth work having already, and fervently, imagined my life with Disney Studios, the Rolling Stones and Mother Teresa. Pride was not so much the issue as was my appetite for dreaming big. And what I lacked in wisdom, I made up for in chutzpah by envisioning joining the camps of the most famous mouse, the most famous touring band and the most famous nun in the world.

Funny thing, though. I couldn't have ended up further from Mickey, Mick or Mother than I did—at age 23, guess-working my way through the uncharted waters of street-savvy teenagers in the tumultuous and unglamorous northwest end of Canada's largest metropolis, with very few resources and even fewer assurances.

The notion to start what was commonly coined as a "drop-in" for "street kids" was as thorny around its wording then as it is now—or as I prophesy, it always will be. What does "drop-in" imply? (Unstructured, uninteresting, unintentional?) What does "street kids" imply? (Troublemakers, delinquents, brats?) While the trend to create youth drop-ins really sprung to life across North America in the early 1990s, and could almost be described as an epidemic phenomenon—and a statistically unsuccessful trend—by the new millennium, there were few, if any, templates to follow in 1987 for titles, structures or protocols. But interestingly, even now, with countless similar ventures having transpired over the past quarter of a century—from church basements to superstructures, with some funky variations vibing as much disco club as coffee house—the perfect moniker and model remains elusive.

All these matters notwithstanding, my home church (Weston Park Baptist Church) partnered with Youth Unlimited and gambled that I might have as much of a clue as anyone about how to design and unpack something workable for teenagers in Weston.

And while I really didn't, the truth is, my guess was as good as anyone else's. And much to their credit, both the church and Youth Unlimited were on their own brave learning curve in stepping out in this trusting manner.

Thus, on paper anyway, Frontlines was initially designed and described as a place "where all teenagers are welcomed, regardless of ethnic or religious background," and "geared to the social, mental, physical and emotional areas of life." Somewhat dated language now, to be sure, but authentic at heart and contemporary at the time. But not to be undersold by the big bad world outside our doors, or to miss out on words to squirm by in years to come, this jingly phrase was added to the mix: "In sharp contrast to some of the influences pressuring young people into anti-social behaviour, Frontlines strives to provide a steadying influence." A collective of educators, youth mentors, pontificators, community cheerleaders and critics met to word and re-word this very big branding for a very small project. And in the end, for the most part, the church liked it, Youth Unlimited liked it, and the community at large liked it. The funny thing is for the years I ran it, I never heard a single teenager describe it as anything but "a drop-in for street kids."

For months, my supervisors, makeshift advisors, closest friends and anyone else I could beg aboard patched up a beaten little storefront attached to the side of a motorcycle shop. Occasionally, community leaders, police officers and locals would poke their heads in the door to see what we were doing and ask why we were doing it. This seldom helped matters as far as I was concerned as no one seemed even mildly impressed or convinced. And if gearing up was not anxious enough, opening day's first young guest was just plain painful. A local long-haired rocker kid threw the door open, stepped in and stopped, put his hands on his hips, scanned the place from left to right, looked me square in the eyes and snorted, "This will never work," turned and walked away.

As it is, that snarky kid would be in his forties now, and Frontlines has grown to be what I never could've made it or imagined it, by way of a series of excellent directors and boards, including those that keep it thriving even as I write this.

But that's what baby steps are all about. Crawling. Imagining being upright. Moving out of a crawl. Falling after a wobbly step or two and landing on a wet diaper. Bonking your head. Crying. Deciding crawling is easier. And still getting up and going at it again. Guessing that it's possible.

If nothing else, God granted me favour even in guesswork-gone-bad in that I wasn't fired nor was I ever required to stand before a judge and plead my case over any number of, what I liked to simply and nonchalantly call, "little incidents."

For example, there was the "little" moto incident. I was into casual motocross trail riding at the time and convinced the bike shop next door to do some comp work on my engine. Having just had the bike returned from the shop next door, in one of my weaker moments of discretion, I attempted to gain some cool factor by agreeing to teach a 15-year-old how to kick-start the bike, shift into first gear and ride the length of the drop-in. Inside the drop-in, that is. As it turns out, it only takes a millisecond for an inexperienced and over-adrenalized 15-year-old to inadvertently pop the clutch into a screaming wheelie. The end result, once the cloud of blue smoke dissipated, was rug burn severe enough to require a hospital visit, two sprained wrists, a demolished bumper-pool table, a new set of forks for the front end of my bike, and a week of silent terror waiting for an outraged parent to storm through the front doors and tear my head off. But cruel irony spared me, as it does for so many working among those tagged as "high risk"; his parents couldn't have cared less.

CHAPTER 10

Then there was the "little" nail incident. One that I know was just plain wrong of me, but to this very day I still feel awkwardly justified in, hanging on to a rough edge in my soul yet to be buffed and polished. At age 23, I was still actually "relevant" in the eyes of the teenagers I was working with. Dressed similar, listened to and truly loved the same music, ate at the same fast food joints, and for the most part, was still young enough to live and dream out of my naïveté. My connecting point with most of the young people I was able to bond with was almost always by way of music. Thus, if there was one tipping point in labelling the original Frontlines in any specific manner, it was that local kids eventually tagged it as a "rock drop-in."

We spent hours debating the current and most important teenage rock matters at hand—whether Steve Earle and Neil Young could truly be called "rockers;" why Rush were Canadian icons whether you liked them or not; how Metallica suddenly made all the other current bands look like posers; how AC/DC could make the same three chords sound great, album after album; and why the newest band on the scene—Guns N' Roses—was destined for legendary status so early. It was my dream job. I loved these conversations with the same passion that I hated the ones I had to have with an endless stream of Christian youth workers who hated my approach and jabbed relentlessly that anything but Christian rock and pop music was detrimental.

But those rock conversations were all just part of the big picture. The goal was always to press these dialogues to a finer point of finding what in all of this resonated with young people. The hurts and joys, dreams and nightmares, and ploys that loomed or surfaced. Then taking it all one step further. To play it, to drum it, to sing it, to scream it, to gather over it, and maybe, just maybe, as unlikely as it seemed, to find healing in it.

"Music can change the world because it can change people."—Bono

Inevitably, Frontlines' first core group of volunteers were musicians and musician wannabes. After-school jam sessions, Friday night free-for-alls, and field trips to music stores were the only programs I worked at for the first two years. Kids who'd never picked up a drumstick in their lives lost themselves to beats they had no idea they were carrying. Curbside guitar heroes and sidewalk vocalists sprang from wallflowers and ne'er-do-wells. And a whole whack of kids with great talent and no resources or outlet found a nesting place.

And the little nail incident? If nothing else, it represented the passion I had for the whole thing. I had scored some very decent equipment and a house PA system to facilitate the only "how tos" I felt truly comfortable with at the time. But our little rental facility was very shy on other assets, such as security. What we did have was what we created. Our landlord wanted nothing more than our money and no problems, and was willing to offer nothing more than taking our money and providing no solutions. So we gated the windows ourselves with construction rebar and hook nails and created drawbridge-esque back door jambs with eight foot two-by-fours.

But one month into our first autumn mini-concert series, we were robbed. The culprits bashed their way through an old hideaway window we had boarded over and insulated behind the furnace. The speakers were gone, the guitars were gone, the drums were gone. Gone, gone, gone. I was furious! I stormed and stomped around the space, hollering like an overindulged rock star who'd found brown M&Ms in his candy bowl when his rider clearly demanded no browns. But much more than angry, I was heartbroken.

Small potatoes now as I look back on it—but all the same, there is something very special about young youth workers who live in the zeal of their endeavours and efforts. If it's truly a matter of passion rather than pride, it's something I think requires more celebration than mentoring. In-the-now, I might guess that many a youth work specialist and youth culture guru would build better systems and guidelines for learning from such an experience.

But...hmph. Sometimes I think it's okay to just be ticked off. And that's what I was.

In short order, a police report was completed, the break-in's entry point was double-boarded and secured, our insurance company replaced the snatched equipment, and young people were making music, near-music, and lots of amplified noise once again.

Ideally, this would be a nice little story about fervour and growing pains in youth work. But just a few short weeks later, the same entry point was battering-rammed for a second time, and all the replacement equipment and gear was stolen. Gone, gone, gone again!

"Ticked off" doesn't even begin to express the tip of the iceberg that was my emotions. I was livid. But being livid in high-risk youth work now is not like being livid in high-risk youth work back then. It's much harder now to know what to do with those emotions beyond sounding them out among God, your direct supervisor and your peers.

For the record, I think protocols are indeed a very fine thing. As are statutes of limitations, policies, procedures and best practices. God bless those who create them, use them, and are spared because of them. Scribe it, scrub it, teach it, preach it, speak it, riff it and repeat it, and make sure no one leaves unless they have signed on the dotted line. Truly, every ounce of energy spent making sure youth workers and youth are simultaneously safe and safe-guarded gets my vote. If for no other reason than I'm the dad of two teenagers. How could I wish for or want anything less?

But with all that said, I am so glad that my green years in youth ministry came before the supersonic and high-tech age of personal and professional coaching expertise, occupational instruction for the psyche and soul, Zen-like mentoring, and über-refined church-and-charitable legalese. I never would've made it.

Just not enough guesswork.

Shockingly, the insurance company came through with still more replace-ments—along with some serious investigation and a notice of "final claim avail-able." This time, we triple-boarded and bolted the crime scene's entry point, and even had the police inspect the work. But once all these things were complete, I was (A) unconvinced by anything that wasn't a bricks-and-mortar resolve, and (B) too bothered to not decree some form of revenge on anyone so brazen as to go at it one more time.

Like a pea-brained caveman with a club and a dispute, I singularly decided on one more "good" idea. Didn't tell my supervisor at Youth Unlimited. Didn't tell the church. Didn't tell the volunteer board. Didn't tell the police. And didn't think twice about not telling a soul. I pounded 200 two-inch nails through a half-inch-thick piece of plywood, turned it upside down with the spikes facing up, and placed it below the boarded window well, behind the furnace.

It wasn't long before the music started again, and word of our new equip-ment reached the street.

I will never forget the contrasting emotions of guilt and satisfaction the day I entered Frontlines' back door, having seen that somehow, someone had sledgehammered their way through our radical repairs yet again, and I rushed inside. I ran through the tiny office area to the drop-in, only to find every single piece of equipment exactly where it had been left the evening before. Then I knowingly sauntered over behind the furnace to find my payback-board of nails completely covered in blood, feverishly kicked several feet away from where it had been placed. Whoever hang-dropped through the forced-entry hole had landed with both feet on the spikes, and had to sort out their impaled agony and escape without making a peep.

A few local kids popped by on the way to school while I was scanning the scene and playing it out in my mind. Without asking a single question, they stared for a few seconds, put two and two together, and raced off buzzing like bees.

By the time after-school drop-in opened, the nail board was long gone, the wall was refashioned, and I just smiled and walked away from any questions asked.

I can't imagine there is a professional drop-in worker, youth worker, or street outreach worker alive that would publicly say I did the right thing. Or privately, for that matter. But for the rest of my time at Frontlines, we never had a single item burgled, bartered for, or even looked at sideways again. Not ever.

Ah, guesswork.

But that's all these little incidents were. Guesswork. Just guesswork. And admittedly, if not yet repentantly, bad guesswork at that. Ultimately, that just isn't good enough. That kind of guesswork is highly self-indulgent. Good guesswork is not about choosing to gamble. It's not about frivolously playing games of chance or seeking out risk as folly or revenge. The stakes are too high to have us treat one another as a lottery. No important relationship can survive a "win some / lose some" attitude. Good guesswork—the kind that matters—is mindful, not mindless. Good guesswork is prayerful, longs for a sign from on high, looks at things from as many directions as possible, works to be informed, and still and always, never loses sight of what matters most when push comes to shove—people's hearts. It is dug deep in the humility of not knowing, watered by the hope of doing what's best, and sunned by the notion that any possible consequences are worth it. And in the end, guesswork is not good and is nothing more than an emotional tax, unless it thrives under the cool shade of courage. The courage ultimately required to make a decision.

And if I didn't know it before, or was never to know it again, I surely knew it once upon a time when three unforgettables tested the constitution of my word and the fortitude of my guesswork. Ones I knew only briefly, but profoundly.

There is no soft way to tell this story. And I won't insult you by trying to find it.

When Frontlines began, I struggled daily with keeping the doors closed during school hours. This was guesswork that pained me every single Monday to Friday. I wanted the local junior high and senior high schools (both of which I had attended) to receive Frontlines in a positive light. Giving kids a place to hang out when skipping classes would surely be a black eye on that endeavour.

At the same time, meeting those kids at those times was what I wanted to do most. I've been accused of being an "enabler" throughout my entire adult life. Feeding people who should get jobs and buy their own food. Clothing people who beg for money and then buy drugs. Spending time with people who should get off the damn sidewalk and do something with their lives. The accusations barely reach me as anything but insulting, no matter where they come from or how they're phrased—mostly because they ultimately imply that I'm more stupid than anything else.

A great many things have changed in my heart and mind over time, including complete backflips and one-eighties over all kinds of theological matters, ideologies and humanity issues. But my feelings on this matter have never ever wavered.

To reach out to people when they need it most is not guesswork. It's just the right thing to do.

Sure, sure, we don't want to pry. Don't want to say or do the wrong thing. Don't want to interfere, get involved, make waves, blah-blah-blah. Hey, I get that! You would know in very short order whether I wanted you dabbling in my personal business, thought you should bug out, or if you had crossed a line. And the older I get, the wider and more pronounced those lines get.

But as our ever-changing tech-and-media-happy society continues to nudge gentle people into obscurity and prod brash people into the limelight, the world needs tender voices more than ever. Tender voices. Not weak voices. There's a big difference. The tender people I have known who truly shape the world in godly ways are strong in character and brave enough to attempt navigating the most important lines in the sand. The one between hypersensitivity and sensitivity. The one between motive and spirit. And surely the one between bad guesswork and good guesswork.

While I was clearly not one of those people, God had put the desire in me to work toward becoming like them. Mostly because it was then just as it is now. Those were—and are—the people I adore and appreciate most, and who have been my lifeboat.

Two p.m. on a blustery and frightfully cold Wednesday afternoon. Sixty minutes after we'd closed the lunch hour drop-in time, there was a pounding on our storefront windows. Outside, three boys I didn't technically know, but my soul felt like it did.

These guys were rough. The real deal. Not smokin' and cursin' rough. The smokin' and cursin' kids who thought themselves rough and tough were a dime a dozen. They still are. Showboating blades and baggies of pot, giggling over hangovers and porn. Being rough in a rough neighbourhood is nothing particularly novel. It gets old really fast. There are only two things that are. One—being sweet and kind. Two—being the kind of rough these guys were.

They weren't out to impress anyone. Their egos didn't need that tough guy attention or flattery. They had seen enough childhood pain to leapfrog over street corner hardness. These were the guys I would see making midnight transactions in the dark shadows behind the motorcycle shop when I was closing the drop-in. These were the guys whom people feared because they barely said anything, not because they said too much. These were the guys who weren't spending any time trying to figure out which adults to trust because they had decided there were none. These were three guys who had already begun the journey into the unforgiving world of gangs.

The take on gangs in Toronto, like in any city, depends on who you ask. Info then was just as it is now. Usually the people who talk about it the most, or the loudest, know it the least. The silent ones have the inside scoop. Quite often, because they are, in fact, on the inside. Still, I had a few local officers give me the lowdown from their perspective from time to time. And the word I had on it was that the turf gangs around Weston were fragmented and upstarts, for the most part. Not organized enough to create a scene, but definitely generating enough of a stir for concern. To that end, I never really knew what was going down with these three guys but was certain they were always lurking in parking lots and alleyways in the wee hours, often getting in and out of slow moving vehicles, and that no one I knew really knew them or had any interest in messing with them.

What I did know was this. They were young. And they were headed for trouble.

As I walked toward the front windows, I could see them chuckling at the puzzled look on my face. I turned the bolt and the wind all but opened the door for me.

"Hey, freezing out here," one of them spoke in a low voice.

I will never forget that the sentence ended there. He—or they—never actually asked to come in, but stood and waited for me to reply by inviting them in out of the cold. Hopeful, but no assumption. Quite polite. And very intriguing.

Kids were always banging at the front windows during school hours, and I was always shooing them away. But I was so fascinated that these three guys had showed up and were talking to me that I didn't even consider not bringing them inside. They followed me into the little office space behind the stage and sat side-by-side on my desk. The whole thing was wonderfully awkward. I didn't know what to say to them, and they didn't know what to say to me. They just wanted out of the cold, and no one else would let them loiter.

Finally, in an attempt to break the tension, I began babbling. Just going with the whole crazy weather thing that brought them to my doorstep. But it was ridiculous. I was many sentences into a very yappy account of the harsh weather and forecast ahead when I realized I was messing up. They weren't even bothering to hum and haw in acknowledgement of my one-sided conversation. It was clear they were enduring my feeble chat just to stay warm. This opportunity was not going to come again, and especially if I didn't drop myself into a gear that gave this precious bit of time some room to breathe. So I stopped, right in the middle of some tiresome sentence, and said, "Y'know, this isn't common. I don't usually let kids in during school hours."

And all three raised their heads and smiled, reminding me in an instant of what the difference is between being talked at and being talked to.

I continued. "Why aren't you guys in class?"

You get a rare handful of special moments in life that never leave you. Not moments that are about memories. There are boatloads of those, if you can keep them straight. But moments that are about feeling something. A handful of somethings that feel like nothing else. Sitting in that rustic little office with these three complete strangers, awaiting a response, was one of those somethings.

I had already shut myself down to gain some respect, so I was determined to wait on a response without repeating myself. But never had I been so baffled by facial expressions, sighing or body language. I couldn't tell if they were going to break out laughing or break my legs. There were a few harmless snorts, a few head nods back and forth between them, and several more uncomfortable moments of silence.

Then finally, one of them—Todd—leaned forward a few inches and spoke like a modern-day James Dean:

"We're f*ck-ups."

He took back his inches and we all sat silent again.

In the end, after a few false starts, I was able to crack the nut. These three boys had, in fact, been in class that afternoon. But the teacher didn't want them there and gave them the heave-ho in his own special way. I can only imagine the distraction their presence and attitude would've cost a classroom on an ongoing basis. I might guess that completed homework assignments and classroom participation were not making the grade. But as they told it, these were not the reasons they were sent away.

On this day, whatever contempt had built up had fused with some kind of authoritative rage, and the teacher simply pointed to the back of the class and said, "You three are f*ck-ups. Get out."

And they did.

I wonder how many people will look in the mirror today and tell themselves they are "f*ck-ups"? How many people will fall asleep in tears tonight believing it's so? How many rich people can't buy their way out of it? How many drinks or hits does it take to forget it? How much success will it take to defuse it, and how much failure to own it, wear it and roll around in it until it's all you know? Are you holding this book in your hand right now and feel that I'm speaking directly to you?

No one needs to be told it. No one needs to be sold it. It's a lie.

And while this is where the love of God is begged on most, it's also where it can be counted as faithful. Surely few supplications find and break the heart of God quite like the wounded plea of a self-proclaimed "f*ck-up."

"The Lord is close to the brokenhearted" (Psalm 34:18, NLT).

Those three boys came and spent time with me every day after that for the next two weeks during the time slot of the class they were banished from. I heard street language I had never heard before or even knew existed, and secret stories too vile to repeat. Bit by bit, they dropped their guard and even began exploring some of the equipment.

I cherished every moment. I learned about things you sure can't learn in school. And one of the boys actually had a bit of talent around six strings and an amplifier. The dual unleashing of trust and cautious play ultimately resulted in one more conversation I did not anticipate, and was not prepared for. One afternoon, they were trying to jam as a threesome while I was taking a call. It sounded horrible, but fun. I was still on my call when everything went silent. I could hear them talking for several minutes, but could not make out what they were saying. Finally, Todd came to me.

"We want to start a band."

Some people believe that every teenager should play on a sports team. Others believe every teenager should be in a youth group. Of course, good grades and family traditions are standard "shoulds." But if not a "should," then at least a "could." I wish every teenager could start a band. Every gangster, every cheerleader, every church kid, every every-other-thing kid, every single one.

Nothing built my confidence, filled me up, taught me about the give-and-take of teamwork or juiced my creativity and enthusiasm when I was a teenager like playing in a garage band, trying to get it out of the garage. No matter how rotten we were.

Frontlines was very good at the band thing by this time. Not just around equipment and space, but around learning, creating community, freedom of expression and creativity. We took some hard hits on the matter, not always seemingly "in sharp contrast to some of the influences pressuring young people into anti-social behaviour." But the end result was always, always, always worth it. As such, there were very few ground rules, but the music could never be about oppressing or hurting people. Dozens of Friday night bands started and ended at Frontlines. Along the way, some future success stories and even a star grew out of the Frontlines camp. This special trio was just one of the motley crews who always made it worthwhile.

The guys had it all worked out, jazzed by something safer than the street lives they'd been leading.

As though there was nothing to discuss, Todd continued: "We want to call ourselves the F*ck-Ups!"

Ah...guesswork.

They wanted that name, and would not budge on it. Satirical ownership and a contrite nod to anyone who might anticipate anything less of them. I thought it was far too crude, quite ingenious, and just plain impossible at my end. And then to make matters worse, they wanted to plan a concert for a Wednesday afternoon, poignant homage to the day they were banished from class. And they would not budge on that either. They were killing me.

I barraged them with an endless list of concerns and petitions:

"We can't put up posters with that name on it. You gotta think of another name. I'll have everyone at my throat."

"This whole you-being-here-during-school-hours is a secret, remember? No Wednesday afternoon gigs!"

"Who's gonna come on a Wednesday afternoon anyway? And if they do, it will just be a big problem!"

I kept at it.

"No, no, no."

But they had their street demeanour down cold. The vibe that had kept them intact in the back alleys was no different in this unanticipated negotiation. No spouting off. No voices raised or arms flailed. They just stayed the course, and Todd did most of the talking. This is how it's got to be. This is why.

Guesswork, shmesh work. At the end of the day, they just wore me down. I wasn't bullied into it. I wasn't hypnotized passive-aggressively. I was just worn down by persistence and guesswork.

But there were a few deal breakers. Small bones tossed my way to pacify me. For countless reasons, there could be no posters. Agreed. The whole thing had to end before the after-school crowd arrived. Agreed. And no surprise gang stuff of any kind. Agreed.

For two weeks, they came in faithfully and practised. Never when we were technically "open." They sounded awful, really awful, and the whole thing felt worrisome at best. It wasn't until the week of the gig that I asked, "Who's coming to this, anyway?"

Todd: "Wednesday afternoon f*ck-ups, like us."

Uh oh.

Two p.m. on a grey and chilly Wednesday afternoon—exactly five weeks from the hour they first darkened my door—they plucked and tapped their way slowly to the first warbly chord of Iggy and the Stooges' "Dirt," followed by the telling opening lyrics:

"Ooh, I been dirt. And I don't care."

Gathered in the room were dozens of teenagers I didn't know and had never seen inside the drop-in before. It was remarkable.

A clan of truancy offenders? No doubt. A tribe of young ones on the cusp of troubled times more perilous than they knew? Perhaps. A gathering of high school f*ck-ups?

Absolutely not. Anything but.

To this day, from sports teams to camp staffs to kumbaya youth groups, I have never seen a group of young people so harmonious in their solidarity and identity.

Todd stood at the microphone before the final song of their short and very messy mini-concert. I leaned against a giant space spider video game at the back of the room while he thanked me in front of his grubby peers, trying to hide any emotion, guessing that it would be the uncoolest thing imaginable. But then he continued in what can only be described as a radical moment in time.

The room fell completely silent but for the buzz and tinny reverb of poorly grounded amplifiers in waiting. He looked at his buddies on the tiny stage, then looked at the collection of dropouts and misfits that had assembled. He scanned the room, looking into the faces of the grubby mob, one at a time, in reverence. The room was electric with sorrow and glory, all rolled into one.

Finally, Todd spoke.

"We don't have to be what they think we are."

And the room remained silent for a few moments, then all of a sudden exploded with applause and cheering. He didn't have to explain the "what" or expand on who "they" were. Everyone in the room knew exactly what he was saying. Not by way of head knowledge, rebellion or street comprehension, but by way of their souls. Because in the end, it wasn't really about the "what" or the "they." It was about the "we."

CHAPTER 10

It wasn't planned. It wasn't scripted. And it sure wasn't guesswork. It was simply truth. And it was heroic.

I didn't have Todd's courage when I was his age. Not even close. And I don't have it now. I would've found myself guessing on it, for sure. It's funny how we choose our heroes. Ask any adult about what they admire in people and one by one, piece by piece, they will begin to verbally construct their ideal role model and hero. Attaching qualities, characteristics, mannerisms and skills like body parts on a Mr. Potato Head. It's a conversation that I find most often crosses the line between interesting and crazy-making within seconds, as pride almost always seeps in, just in the telling, as the "whats" turn into long self-involved "whys."

So the older I get, the fewer heroes I have. I admire more and more people all the time. Some, I admire to the point that I could burst trying to describe them. But they aren't my heroes. The truth is my standards for heroism keep diminishing. I've spent my adult years spurred on by the notion of goal setting and vision casting. Surrounded by motivators and role models in this arena who have reached heights of success incomprehensible to me. People I admire greatly! But they aren't my heroes.

My heroes are the Todds. It would be easy to squeeze in a warm and fuzzy ode to the anti-hero here and say that's why. But that would be nothing new. And it's just not why. From Shakespeare to *Mad Magazine*, billboards to bubblegum comics, there's always been a wide-eyed esteem for a good bad boy, a free-spirited wild child and a rebel without a cause. So what? That stuff is interesting, intriguing and most often captivating. But not heroic. Todd lives in my memory as heroic because he knew what it meant to find a moment, make it special and share that moment without pretense.

My heroes don't love the past or lust for the future. They live in the moment. Nothing is harder than being in the moment and truly making the most of it. It takes an abandon like no other to not be distracted by worry or preoccupied by anticipation. Not to yearn for what was or wish for what's coming. It takes a special courage that sees others over self. It takes a special humility to be completely present and completely selfless, simultaneously. It makes the best memories and inspires the greatest hope. It's beautiful as it is. It's treasure found but once. It's life-giving. It's life-receiving. It's abundant living. It's the New Testament.

Todd tried to say a few more words, but his fans for the day wouldn't have it. They just kept on cheering. True to form, he did not press the matter, and the band banged out the Rolling Stones' "You Can't Always Get What You Want" to close, completely mutilating one of rock's simplest opuses.

GUESSING SO

The crowd of Wednesday afternoon strangers departed with the bad boys turned bad band, all before the afternoon school bell rang. Just as bargained. And they never came back. None of them. Not ever. I was shocked. And sad. Sad to this day about it.

Throughout the seasons that followed, I would spot them here and there, usually individually, skulking and creeping around the shadowy fringes of the community in some sketchy fashion. Occasionally, I would catch a nod or a smile if we made eye contact. I always figured it was the equivalent of a hug from this faction, and received it as such. But in the end, I had no idea what became of them. No one lasts long living the streets like that. It's only a matter of time. You either go deeper into the darkness or come out into the light.

I like to imagine they found their way out of the sordid world they had come to know and be part of. That Todd's words rang true beyond the moment they so magically hung in the air, and that he—and they—found other ways to make messy music in life that, while imperfect, may have been nourishing and meaningful. That their little set list's opening and closing lyrics stirred restlessly in their hearts. That they knew they weren't dirt. That they cared. And that there were days that they were blessed to both get what they wanted and what they needed.

But if I were a betting man, would I gamble that this was so?

No. It's just my best guess.

"It's like the blind leading the blind."

It's a pretty common statement, used endlessly to describe incompetence in a plural sense. I threw it out there as a straight line while my friend and I watched from afar as two deaf teenagers bumbled their way through fixing a rickety old shed door. Inexperienced young people serving on the Ontario Camp of the Deaf's maintenance team, taking on a simple task. As soon as the words came out of my mouth, there was a dramatic pause, and then we both burst out laughing, recognizing the great irony.

Eventually, the shed door was repaired without any outside assistance, and the two deaf boys felt a sense of accomplishment, having learned a new thing or two along the way. For sure, my unbeknownst sarcasm didn't help them in any way. It also went unheard, so it didn't hurt them either, I suppose. But it did wear at me, and the phrase has stuck in my mind in a different manner ever since. I just can't help but think that if I were blind, I would hate to hear sighted people throw around that metaphor as a, well, as a visual.

Words. Ugh. Nowhere does danger loom like it does in the long weeds of words. And among them, labels and names are the ultimate booby traps.

Very few schoolyard jingles have remained as timeless, or as completely untrue, as this:

"Sticks and stones may break my bones, but names will never hurt me."

Nope. I just don't buy it. But I do believe there is a revised saying that is closer to the truth:

"Sticks and stones may break my bones, but words do permanent damage."

We've all survived a great many physical bumps and bruises in life, perhaps even sticks and stones, if not much worse, while remaining perpetually wounded by sharp and painful words. When I was eight years old, I cracked my head open into a great bloody mess and was rushed to the hospital. When I think back on it, I laugh. But that same week, a bully in grade 3 teased me about my cheap running shoes in front of the entire class and I can recall it like it was yesterday. And when I do, I feel it like I was that very same embarrassed little boy again.

Yeah. Words. Just words. But ugh.

I have been both the abused and the abuser too many times. And just when I think I have it licked, as receiver or giver—a tough enough skin to survive it, an easy enough disposition to roll with it, an astute enough intellect to speak safely, or a thoughtful enough character not to joke too far—I blow it. Again and again. And that's just in the everyday how-do-you-do-ness of life, where casual conversations and riffing with buddies should be simplest. Move the process forward to correctly identifying people groups or classifications and speaking publicly, and yikes, the drama and danger can be mesmerizing.

The only thing I am sure of is this: If we expect one another to get it all right, we should anticipate spectacular disappointment all the way to the grave. Because even the most gracious and thoughtful among us could never keep up with the parade of words that pass or fail when it comes to speaking aloud.

Everyone from punk rockers to evangelicals wants to make sure, if nothing else, that you get their distinction and distinctness correct. Passionate that there will be no lumping together, misinterpretation or misrepresentation when it comes to speaking of "me." No painting with the same brush. No assumptions. We all picnic or protest beneath a number of banners that separate us by way of social, cultural and spiritual mathematics. This plus this plus this equals me. Get it? If not, you'll then most likely be schooled further by subtraction—I'm not this, or this, or this.

Some of us—me, very much included—just need to lighten up. Spare the world from the distinctions we want poeticized, and get on with living out the distinctions that matter most. Especially around the self-indulgence of choice-based categories. There are many more important matters around precious lives that have been shaped by non-choices that are truly worthy of our attention and understanding.

Even as I consider this portion of this chapter, I wonder how rapidly the very words I choose to use here will be considered passé, unacceptable, or downright offensive to readers just a few years after this book's first printing.

The year before I was enrolled in a college developmental service worker course, hard to believe, but the graduating class received their diplomas as mental retardation counsellors. While the telling of this alone makes it sound like I went to college several ancient lifetimes ago, by the time I attended my first class in that same course, the student body was already in shock at the stone-age terminology that had just preceded us.

All of this was just around the time when the healthy mainstream thought they'd finally found a safe word to dignify a world full of people that were one, some, or all of these: hard to understand, difficult to categorize, awkward to gather around, easy to pity.

That word?

"Special."

Sigh. Too deep an ocean to explore in a quick swim, but here are a few of the cresting waves.

"Handicapped" became a no-no not too long ago, and handicap parking permits became accessible parking permits. Many of the people with such permits are now (well, as I currently write this anyway) PWD ("persons with disabilities"). That's kind of special, even if this too will all change in time.

Those who were "physically disabled" are now "mobility impaired." Uh huh, that's special too.

"Neurodiverse" trumps "autistic" for some. Who knew? Either way, special again.

"Emotionally disabled" is the new "bipolar," and "manic depressive" has been couched as "mood disorders." Very special indeed. Ah, but few emotionally disabled people would ever want or allow their disorder to be corralled into the same category as other "special" people. And that *is* the point.

I have come to know a great many people with cerebral palsy who've told me their greatest suffering actually comes from people's unknowingness and misinterpretation of them, needlessly fearful of their involuntary motions or motor conditions that impact body movements and speech.

The whole thing is akin to saying all food is the same. Bring a vegan a steak and you'll understand it's not so. Dish out tofu to a steak-lovin' cowboy and be ready to hear about it. Serve a peanut butter sandwich to someone with peanut allergies and you will be reminded in no uncertain terms that food is not just food. Each item is uniquely palatable, looks different, grows different or is of its own distinctive recipe. "Food" is not generally considered special so much as each unique food item is, for what it is.

While well enough intended, ultimately the word "special" seemed to identify people as anything *but* special, especially when it conveniently fronted the term "special needs." In the end, it did little more than identify them as different and unusual.

It's a no-win proposition, to be sure. I actually grew up using the word "special" in this way as a term meant to dignify others, while recognizing my own ignorance to whatever they were challenged with, impaired by, or whatever in-the-moment phraseology was best. Special Olympics Canada is "dedicated to enriching the lives of Canadians with an intellectual disability through sport." Wow. Who can criticize that? I am totally on-board! But case in point: How much of the general population has not taken notice that the Paralympics are not at all, or even remotely, the same thing? The Canadian Paralympic Committee is dedicated to "develop[ing] sport and sport-related opportunities for people with a physical disability, so that they can fulfill their personal potential and fully participate in their community." Indeed, both are very special. But alas, back to the food thing. These are apples and oranges.

So then, if the words can never be perfect, and we can never be perfect with them, where on earth do we take all this from here? If nowhere else, we can take it to heart. In the modern age of instant information, most of us are only a click away from catching up with contemporary words and wisdom on such matters. It just takes a few seconds and a bit of sincere interest. And then, as is always the case, whatever words come out will not matter so much as how they are said.

There is a life trifecta that is always the best bet, with the odds always in your favour:

Thoughtfulness always rules the day.
Best attempts are always good medicine.
Humility always speaks louder than words.

And that is what it takes. One, two and three. No less. No way. Because the complexities are endless.

"Dual diagnosis" can mean anything from two conditions such as diseases and syndromes existing simultaneously, to alcohol abuse combined with social anxiety. That's a long reach for one bit of terminology. But "dual disabilities" is yet another thing: a term used on many fronts, including speaking to the issue of compounded physical and mental challenges or impairments. In my younger years of service and community among deaf children and adults, we held summer camp sessions called "Special Camp" for what we called "deaf plus"—usually meaning they were deaf compounded with any number of additional "special needs." And the plain truth is this: If ever the word "special" fit anywhere, it was here, if for no other reason than for me, personally, these camp experiences were some of the most extraordinary and life-changing I would ever know.

Of all the unanticipated things to occur, it was among the deaf that I was really introduced to the blind. Dually disabled, deaf-plus, or whatever you might call them, we just lovingly called them by their names, and loved them as such.

I will never forget the first time I met a deaf-blind person and her interpreter sitting at the top of the camp hill and became entranced with tactile sign language, fascinated by the manual alphabet, signing by touch and hand-over-hand communication, all at rapid speed. To this day, it is nothing less to me now than it was then. Shocking and beautiful.

Over the years, we had more than a couple of wonderful young deaf staff with diagnosed conditions that would gradually steal their sight, leaving them legally blind within years. The heartache of imaging it was overwhelming.

Glass eyeballs that were removed at night, skin fusions over entire eye sockets, on and on and on. By the time I had experienced several years at the camp, the school for the deaf, and a multitude of institutions and group homes, I had come to know a great many people living blind by way of non-blind-specific venues.

And just by the time I thought I had experienced it all, I met a remarkable boy who was deaf, autistic and blind. Just extraordinary. Lost in his own little world, he would light up by way of his own measure of tactile stimulation and repeat behaviour. He kept a few little two-inch lengths of yarn in his pocket, and once seated comfortably with his legs crossed, he would take one out, tilt his head back and lay it across his nose. Then, manifesting a skill that would wow Houdini, he would curl out his bottom lip and blow from side to side, making the piece of yarn dance back and forth in the air, an inch above his brow. For five and ten minutes at a time, without ever letting the yarn drop, ending by very strategically softening his breath until it landed back on his nose. He would then place the yarn back in his pocket. Then always, he would give a little chuckle, pleased with what he'd felt and done—almost knowingly glib that he could do what others couldn't, and suspecting that we were watching him in awe. His own tiny, intimate, obscure and magic moments dancing with dynamite.

But it wasn't until I was nearing the end of writing this very book (literally weeks before submitting the manuscript to my publisher) that I was gently and profoundly schooled in how to celebrate from a whole new paradigm, thanks to an unassuming blind woman on her own journey of faith.

On day nine of a 15-day voyage that began in Cairo, Egypt, crossed the Sinai Desert, and ended in Jerusalem, Israel, the group I was with was visiting the

CHAPTER 11

Mount of Beatitudes Church, overlooking the breathtaking northwestern shore of the Sea of Galilee.

Designed by famed Italian architect Antonio Barluzzi, and built by Franciscans in 1938 to commemorate Jesus' most famous discourse (the Sermon on the Mount), this Roman Catholic church's eight sides represent the eight beatitudes, also shown in Latin in the upper windows. The central altar is a splendid arch of alabaster and onyx, surrounded by depictions in the mosaic floors of the seven virtues (justice, charity, prudence, faith, fortitude, hope and temperance).

If the ornate stonework, mosaics and cloisters are not enough to overwhelm, this beautiful basilica is surrounded by lush gardens and shaded vistas, and sits atop the mountain range overlooking many of the well-known sights of Jesus' ministry in Galilee. The church, its view and surroundings are collectively considered one of the most gloriously serene locales in the entire Holy Land.

There was more than the eye could take in. Colour and light, human art and God magnificence, all in extravagance. People shook their heads in disbelief and gasped with delight. The elite photographers were in their glory, the hobby photographers were given their moment to shine, and the lightweights like me clicked away without discretion, only knowing that this was not to be missed.

I wandered to the east balcony to lean over the ironwork railing and take in the panorama. While looking upon the landscape, I noticed some creeping figures from the corner of my eye. Two women unlike the other sightseers in our midst. It was a sweet young blind woman tracing the surfaces of the outer wall with both hands as she walked the length of the porch, slowly. At her side was another woman speaking to her in a gentle fluid voice. The blind woman was all but glowing. Every crack she touched was jubilant, and every word from her guide was like a new birth. I turned and watched, so enticed by the two of them that I soon fell into a complete stare. The young blind woman's eyes were sunk deep into her brow, mildly distorting the shape of her face, but only serving to punctuate the wide euphoric smile she wore.

Finally, when their slow pace brought them close by, I stepped toward them, introduced myself and asked where they had come from. The guide was also the blind woman's interpreter, and she bridged our brief conversation softly and reverently. They had come from Poland, on the young girl's dream excursion and pilgrimage of her faith. We spoke for a few minutes, and then the blind woman began to glide forward, anticipating what she might feel or experience in the steps ahead.

I said to her companion, "She is extraordinary. No one else is more captivated than she is."

The guide smiled and responded in accented tones, explaining to me that she saw every word she heard; that she saw everything she touched; that she saw everything she experienced, that "God lets her see what you and I will never see." (I actually wrote the words on the back of a candy wrapper that was in my pocket so I would remember them exactly.)

Words I would suggest may sound too sweet to believe, but for the fact that I saw her with my own two eyes, and there was no mistaking it as so. And downright chilling in this context:

Beatitude number six—"Blessed are the pure in heart, for they will see God."

I had seen the Great Pyramids and Sphinx while riding a camel. I had seen the River Nile from a boat on the River Nile. I had seen the most extravagant riches of the pharaohs. I had seen the Temple of Karnak, Mount Sinai and the desert wilderness of Moses. The gorgeous Gulf of Aqaba, the striking view of the Dead Sea from the top of Masada, and the caves in Qumran where the Dead Sea scrolls were discovered. Over the past week, I had seen them all. But not once did I light up, or see anyone else light up, the way this woman with no sight did.

The guide went on saintly, describing how her young friend would touch every tree, smell every flower, hear every wave and experience every breeze. And here we were, in the most beautiful place we would visit, cameras a clickin', and the one person who truly seemed take it in to the fullest could not "literally" see any of it.

Oblivious to the impact those few moments had on me, the guide departed to catch up with her blind friend, who was reaching the turn toward the next delight awaiting her brilliant imagination.

Soon, our own excursion took us to the shores of the Sea of Galilee. It was calm and still, and most of us tossed aside our shoes and sandals and waded in. But I wanted more. I wanted to see it differently. So I closed my eyes and listened, and felt, and breathed in.

At the sea where Jesus halted a great storm with His words. The sea He walked on. The sea along the hillside where He miraculously fed the 5,000. The same Jesus whose touch soothed and renewed a leper's skin. The same Jesus who mended a paralytic man and liberated an epileptic boy. Ah, the same Jesus who healed the deaf, and the very same who healed the blind. Then healed the blind again. Then went and healed the blind yet again. And yet, interestingly, the one bold enough to compare following false prophets to the blind leading the blind. Wow.

If you don't share my faith, I imagine it's easy to tune out these biblical claims as complete absurdity or happy wishful tales. Be assured, I have had my own days wondering how these claims were on the up and up. But standing in that sea, desperately longing to see God like a blind woman, nothing could've been easier than to believe in a Messiah who brings miracles.

Ten years earlier, when I was thinking through a design and approach to starting up a new Youth Unlimited project called Light Patrol as an outreach that would come alongside homeless youth, I was eager to gather around a motto that could be received by all people, regardless of faith, culture or economic status. And that would also fit idyllically with the heart of my own Christian faith, and that of the agency I worked for. Words that would aptly represent our identity and resonance. These words were chosen, and posted on everything from our mobile bases to our brochures and website:

"Better to light a candle than curse the darkness."

It's a variation on a Chinese proverb that had been adapted and famously used by both John F. Kennedy and Adlai Stevenson in the 1960s.

We just knew there was so much darkness in the lives, surroundings and histories of those we wanted to be good to, and I loved the notion of light piercing that darkness. Until the day I stood on the Mount of Beatitudes, I had never questioned that maxim once. In fact, I had taken the proverb to heart far beyond Light Patrol and had made it my own quiet subtext in life. That when things were sad, bad or dark, I would look for signs of light and celebrate the people who were bringing it. Even on that very trip, through the slums of Cairo, along the segregation walls at the West Bank, and feeling the palpable tensions of clashing faith and politics under a global microscope, there was always someone, or many someones, lighting a candle. People to celebrate.

But the metaphor had always been about sight in my mind. Until I was knee-deep in the Sea of Galilee, denying my eyes. The word "light" in that phrase is a verb, not a noun. An action, not a thing. It is about the doing, the bringing, the creating, the sharing. And in that, I had missed that it may be as much about warmth as it is about light. That for some, bringing and/or receiving light will be feeling something new rather than seeing something new.

And now I love the phrase more than ever.

When and if God sends angels into your presence, you kind of expect them to appear as supernatural beings. More of the walking-through-walls and looking-you-straight-in-the-eyes kind of angels than the blindly-identifying-the-walls-and-never-actually-seeing-you kind. But God never seems to play things that way, or that predictable. Not in my world, anyway.

Funny thing is this: If you asked me to celebrate the blind stranger I met for mere moments in the Promised Land in a single word, I know what it would be.

Special.

The Beatitudes (Matthew 5:3-12)

Blessed are the poor in spirit, for theirs is the Kingdom of heaven.

Blessed are those who mourn, for they will be comforted.

Blessed are the meek, for they will inherit the earth.

Blessed are they which hunger and thirst for righteousness, for they will be filled.

Blessed are the merciful, for they will be shown mercy.

Blessed are the pure in heart, for they will see God.

Blessed are the peacemakers, for they will be called the children of God.

Blessed are they which are persecuted because of righteousness, for theirs is the Kingdom of heaven.

Blessed are you when people insult you, persecute you and falsely say all kinds of evil against you because of me. Rejoice and be glad, because great is your reward in heaven, for in the same way they persecuted the prophets who were before you.

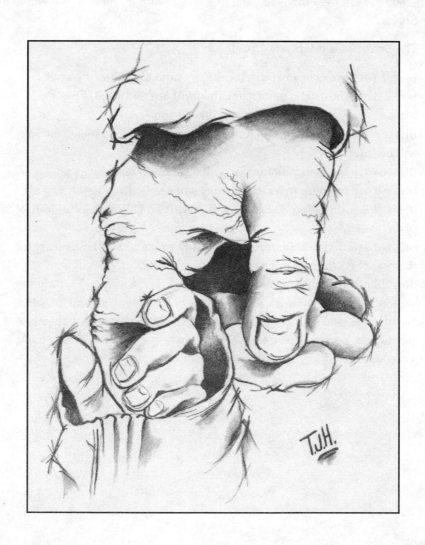

Local transit in the big city is no treat in any season, at any time of the day, as far as I'm concerned. And it's just that much more taxing at the tail end of the suppertime rush hour. Add to it the charcoal sky and last sloppy gasps of a Canadian winter in March, and busing it is hard work, at best.

When my children were wee, one of the popular kids' songs they'd sing was "Wheels on the Bus"—a repetitive ditty that merrily visits the sights and sounds of bus transit, committing each short verse to some small transit reality. In standard versions, the wipers swish, the horn beeps, the motor zooms, the driver gives passenger instructions, a baby cries and a mom shushes. Extended versions often end with the opportunity to use your own name referencing one of the final sounds—in this case, your own voice.

Tim on the bus says, "Let me off! Let me off! Let me off!"

One of the too few days I have chosen not to further my singular carbon footprint on the environment and ride public transit, I found myself loading in with a tired brood of commuters at the bus' departure place, ready to ride it stop-and-go all the way to its final destination, at which point I knew I'd be grumpily singing that final verse under my breath.

The bundled mass shuffled aboard and plopped down without rhyme or reason. Late in line, I was among the last to board. Only a few single seats remained vacant. I walked the stretch of the bus, eyeing my options, met only with the keep-on-looking stares of parka-bound strangers guarding their elbow room and personal space. Having lumbered the full length of the bus, I finally came to the last open seat. I shrugged to the disappointed passengers on either side of it, turned my backside to them and squeezed in.

Bus etiquette is not an exact science. Especially when it's packed. Every inch is like gold, priceless distance from inadvertently touching someone else's body parts, smelling their breath, or being reluctantly interactive with burps, sniffles and sneezes. Appropriate eye contact and casual smiles inexplicably become a mystery the second you pay your fare. Best guesses at the difference between what seems respectful and what seems creepy take on new meaning as you catch a ride with a group of total strangers in tight quarters. There are no hard and fast rules or instructions, but if there were, surely seat selection would require front page status in a guidebook, as one thing is for sure: taking a vacant seat between two adults is always frowned on. More deeply resented still when bodies are double-sized in winter attire.

And then there are the seats that I always seem to land in, seats that run parallel with the bus walls, facing in. An introvert's nightmare. A staging more similar to a sitcom dining room scene where everyone is oddly facing the camera than to any other real-life scenario. And when the bus' belly is stuffed with standing-room-only, these seats allow for the awkward at best butts-and-pelvises-at-eye-level vantage point. A window seat facing forward seems to be the only semi-humane option in a packed city bus, even if akin to a sucker fish pressed against the aquarium wall, watching the fresh-air world go by.

Once seated though, I did what I always do. What most people do. Appear to look at nothing, while really watching everything. I believe that to write the most insightful book ever on Western world sociology, you would need to write the entire thing while riding subway trains, street cars and buses during rush hour. There is nowhere else in the world where dozens and dozens of complete strangers repeatedly sit or stand in unthinkable proximity to one another, entering from and departing for lives whose co-existence on the same planet seems hardly plausible, let alone in the same end of a city. Gangsters and nuns. Dropouts and scholars. Beef eaters and vegans. People headed to crack houses boarding with people headed to PTA meetings. People journeying to ivory towers departing with people journeying to pick up welfare cheques. All of them sharing the same stale air and moments in time. Nothing short of fascinating.

One of the peculiar norms on a busy bus is that while most everyone remains either silent or soft-spoken, there is always one person speaking inappropriately loud. Often, it's someone on a cell phone, oblivious to the best interests of anyone else. Or someone who, while talking to a friend or stranger seated next to them, thinks him or herself funny or entertaining enough that all should hear. Not once can I think of a time that this has been true. This always invokes one of the many cynical missing verses I think I'd add to a grown-up version of "The Wheels on the Bus."

But this was not the case on this bus, on this day. The only loud voice on this ride came from an older man unaware of much more than the mysteries of his own plight.

"Why does it hurt, dammit?" His voice filled the air.

A faint voice would respond, inaudible from where I was seated, followed by a few seconds of quiet, before the next call of alarm.

"I don't understand. I don't like this. Where are we going?"

The rhythm of a frightened senior's voice and a hushed response went on for several minutes at a time. It wasn't until beyond the first few stops, after the standing passengers had departed, that I could see where and who this exchange was coming from. Kitty-corner ahead of me, in a pair of forward-facing seats across the aisle, were an old man and his 30-something-year-old daughter, with a little boy on her lap.

Without any of the small details that define the real wear of a day-in-the-life, the broad strokes of a story that placed mom, son and grandpa in this very place, at this very time, were obvious in short order. The old man would shout out in angst and frustration. His daughter would answer in tired but sweet tones. And the little boy did his best to sit still and not be too much fuss. And anyone within earshot knew what was going down, whether they wanted to or not.

Mom had worked a full day, picked up her boy at daycare, then taken her befuddled dad to the dentist. A long day stitched together by simply doing what needed to be done. No mention of a husband or main man in her life throughout the dialogue, and no ring on her finger, it seemed more than apparent she was flying solo.

Hard-working single moms, bobbing in the sandwich generation, are the unsung backbone of any metropolis. They possess an unheralded stamina, securing the workforce in countless ways, often carrying the entire load of child-rearing, on call for aging parents, and all while living through the stigma and heartbreak of broken relationships and the high cost of personal hopes and dreams coming last. And oh-so-often, unassumingly living through the certainties and uncertainties of the mass commuter system, without a whimper, just as an act of modest means.

There she sat, case in point. The wheels on her bus going round and round, while an old man at her side needed her desperately, a little man on her lap needed her completely, and no man stood with her to share the load. But what was so striking in watching her and listening to her was not what she was missing in that—but what a partner was missing by not taking that place. She was relentlessly gentle and patient, dignified and humble.

CHAPTER 12

As the bus journeyed on, more and more people exited, and it became simpler—though unavoidable—to hear the small family dialogue continue. Emotional multitasking of the miraculous kind. Back-to-back and back again responses to the questions and comments from her dad and son, dad and son, dad and son—all after a drawn-out, grey day stuck on a bus.

"Dad, your mouth hurts because the dentist had to do some work. It will feel better soon."

"We'll be home soon, sweetie, and I will make something. I know you're hungry. I am too."

"Dad, you need to talk a bit softer. No, he didn't hurt you on purpose."

"Yes, I *know* you need five dollars for the school fair tomorrow. I haven't forgotten."

"Dad, we're on the bus home. Remember? I got you on my way from work? The dentist, Dad. We just left the dentist."

"No, we can't afford McDonald's tonight, sweetie. I'm sorry, especially if you need that five dollars tomorrow."

She remained ridiculously composed.

All of it would have been a hero's task in the least, should the same scenario not have included the oppressive nature of extreme dementia. But add to it all the unnerving notion of Alzheimer's disease, and the tiny snapshot of their lives was overwhelming.

While dementia is not a specific disease, many different diseases can cause it. Most commonly, that's Alzheimer's. Often, personalities change and altered states of perception occur. Intense memory loss, an inability to control emotions, and the loss of capacity to problem-solve are common sorrowful effects. It can even make the simplest of everyday life skills, like getting dressed or eating, impossible.

During the last several years of my dear Aunt Marion's life, she was stolen by Alzheimer's. Many may choose to use other more gentle or clinical terms, but I was never able to perceive it as anything different or less than "stolen."

I will never forget my last one-on-one visit with her. During a 30-minute visit over cookies and juice, in a special nursing home, she looked at me, befuddled, and asked me who I was no fewer than 50 times.

When I was a small boy, summers would often include me staying over at her family's home in the country to visit for a few days and play in the barn with my cousin and my brother. Aunt Marion would be up at 5 a.m. with her husband to milk the cows and do the chores, prepare and serve three hot meals every day for her family and the farmhands, keep endless commitments around church and community functions, and somehow sweetly keep us kids in line while we recklessly caused mischief all over the farm. This was Aunt Marion to me. I did not know the new Aunt Marion who spoke like a small child and had no clue who I was, where she was, or what was going on.

This is the astounding thievery of Alzheimer's. That someone could be married for a half century to the same man, raise an entire family, live her entire life in the same small farming community, and, in that moment I was with her, the only thing she knew for sure was that she liked the sugary cookies better than the plain ones being served for snack that day.

Among all the "if there really is a God" questions I have heard in my lifetime, the one that ends with Alzheimer's would surely be among my top three. It mesmerizes me. It terrifies me.

Ah, but the mom on the bus never let me down. I was rooting for her the entire way. The farther we went, the more I became a fan. I would think—*C'mon, don't sigh, don't answer harshly, don't roll your eyes, hang in there, you are my hero.* For 35 minutes straight, stuck in one place, no exits, no reprieves, a champion. My champion. Her plight, my viewing and listening pleasure. Pathetic, beautiful and unavoidable. The awkward and addictive nature of right-time/right-place voyeurism at its best.

And more than anything, smack dab in the middle of it all, my own unjust wishes for the story to bend my way for the moments I was tuned into it. But surely we honour best the families dealing with this unique pain by respecting its realities. The endless hours of frustration and mandatory sacrifice. The days on end of overwhelming grief, and nights filled with unparalleled anxiety. Apologizing to strangers. Overzealously thanking family, friends and acquaintances on someone else's behalf. Tracking good days and bad triggers. Falling asleep in tears. The urgent calls, the harsh words, the public embarrassment, and the sheer pain of remembering when it wasn't so. Even among the bravest of the brave, and kindest of the kind, and the most angelic of the angelic—this too is part of the criminality of Alzheimer's disease.

Finally came a response that jolted me. Not because it seemed out of character—it came in the same, now familiar lovely tones—but because I didn't like it. I was going to lose her.

"Okay, the next stop is ours."

And then, as though we were connected by a tight string, I leaned my head and shoulders forward in dismay, as she leaned her head and shoulders back in sorrow. And I snapped out of my childlike fandom to see the truest face of a broken heart. She angled her head back sharply so her boy and dad couldn't see her face pressed against the window. The fluorescent bus lighting bounced against the backdrop of night on the other side of the glass, causing the pane to be more of a mirror than a window. With a mere 30 seconds to the next stop, she used the time efficiently, allowing a few tears to roll down her cheeks. Not enough time for many. Just the unstoppable ones. The ones that surfaced involuntarily as she mustered her strength for the next leg of the journey. Not a journey from A to B. Or work to home. Or morning to night. But a journey of the soul. One that demands the best of us all. One that puts everyone else first, believing that never wishing we'd done more will one day bring us peace, and will make even the most painful memories bearable.

As the bus began to slow, she covertly wiped her cheeks with her scarf, cleared her throat, looked at them both and smiled.

"Okay, here we go."

And she nudged them both to their feet.

Instantly, gloriously, she was on. In a matter of seconds, she had everyone's coats done up, everyone's hats fixed in place, and everyone's duties assigned. She would carry the grocery bag, her purse, and her son's superhero backpack and take up the rear. Her little boy was to hold grandpa's hand and go forward. And her dad's job was to "be careful."

The little boy reached out his hand and took his grandpa by the finger. Grandpa looked down at him, perplexed, as if to say, "Who are you and what are you doing?" Then he looked up at his daughter, just as befuddled.

"It's okay, Dad," she smiled. "It's okay."

And trusting the tenor of her soft voice over his own confusion and uncertainty, he shuffled forward, and all three stepped out into the next leg of the long journey.

I missed them instantly.

While I can barely imagine what came after, I cannot even comprehend what had once been. His truest life story preserved at best by what he had been bold enough to share while he was still able. Hopefully, some of it captured in a few black and white snapshots, perhaps a few poignant newspaper clippings, and likely a top dresser drawer or an old shoebox cluttered with a few personal treasures and keepsakes. And still, 70-something years of victories and defeats, friends and associates, family squabbles and tender moments, all left somewhere in the foggy past. And a million secrets never told. Some for the better. Some not. The missing verses of his song.

Writing this chapter at age 45 is a poignant part of my own bumpy journey. I am awestruck by how many of my own dear friends are courageously dealing with

Alzheimer's within their own families. For me, the final image of the grandpa being led away by the little boy appears in my head every time I hear their stories. Dignified leaders and visionaries, proud and dedicated patriarchs and matriarchs, committed souls who dreamed, loved, risked and sacrificed greatly, needing now, so-to-speak, to trust whoever takes them by the finger to guide them.

But surely, if there is anything to celebrate in the mix—anything at all to churn from this painful mystery—this is it: love always wins the day. I can think of fewer sounds as tender and sweet as the daughter's unhurried voice. I can think of few sights more precious than the look on the grandson's hopeful face as he took his grandpa's finger—not old enough to really comprehend it all, but old enough to love. What unknown peace exists, even when unrevealed and inexplicable by the afflicted, when the voices and hands of love are steadfast and at work.

We will never know.

But I do know this. As brazen or downright foolish as it is to write about something that is among my own greatest of fears—that if one day I should be there, needing someone to take me by the finger—I will be better in my soul, if not my mind, if they are gentle, patient, forgiving and long-suffering. If they dignify me then, the same way I long to be treated with dignity now. If they grieve the disease and its thieving ways, but celebrate with me the moments I do remember, as infrequent as they may be.

Of all the things I have staked my faith on, none rises above "the greatest of these is love." At times when my own humanity has questioned what it sees as God's absence, knowing that all real love is from God is all that keeps me, and any semblance of my faith, afloat. Surely the truth can be no different for minds that are absent, broken or lost.

At my Aunt Marion's funeral, one of her children shared that while she could not remember who people were or where she was, even as her state worsened she could remember and sing all the great hymns she had learned and loved. Not knowing where they'd come from or how she knew them. I believe it's because they were more in her heart than in her brain. Deeper still, in her soul. No less do I believe that while the old man on the bus may not have detected the voice of his daughter as "his" daughter or the hand of his grandson as "his" grandson, his heart knew better.

And deeper still, his soul.

"Oh, shame"—in big black letters.

"Mr. Nothing"—in big red letters right below it.

It was written across the tailgate of a rusty old two-seater pickup truck passing by us on the outskirts of Johannesburg, South Africa. I don't even really know what it means, but somehow I felt like it was meant for me. I took a picture of it, and keep it taped in the back of the notebook that goes with me everywhere.

It's more than just an obscure statement. It's actually brilliant. It's very difficult to create with just four words a powerful indictment that transcends any singular notion. The allegation reaches further and deeper than the all-too-obvious of a society reeling from the unimaginable legacy of decades of apartheid and the social impact of international sanctions, compounded by the fallout of an urban blight, which includes radical per capita statistics on murder, assault, rape and robbery. The words weren't meant for the mass societal hodgepodge. They cut straight to the heart of the matter— the individual. Not just those who first spin these kinds of maniacal wheels into motion, but those who foster them, and enable them. And perhaps worst of all, those who ignore them. They were meant to be taken personally. And they were.

I felt something very similar visiting Yad Vashem, the Holocaust Martyrs' and Heroes' Remembrance Authority—Israel's living memorial to the Jewish victims of the Holocaust. The largest Holocaust museum in the world, it includes a collection of more than 46,000 audio, video and written testimonies from Holocaust survivors. Likewise, the grounds host the Children's Memorial in an underground cavern, in spectacular remembrance of the million and a half children who perished during the Holocaust, funded by a couple whose own son was murdered in Auschwitz at the age of two.

CHAPTER 13

And I repeatedly feel that same kind of gnawing while walking along 20th Street in Saskatoon, wandering through downtown neighbourhoods in Winnipeg, and passing through central and northern portions of my own province, Ontario—just some of the great many places where there is a large population of First Nations people in Canada. Suicide among Canadian First Nations youth has reached epidemic proportions, occurring five times more often than among non-Aboriginal youth in Canada. As the twentieth century came to an end, suicide among some First Nations communities in Northern Ontario had increased by as much as 400 per cent in a single decade. Profoundly, the rate of suicide is lowest among First Nations communities that have been best able to maintain their own heritage and culture.

It is neither a noble nor intriguing thing to feel sickened and burdened by these matters. If nothing else, I would say these feelings should be considered among the most meagre expectations of humanity. But it is somewhat curious to feel shame over matters in which history and geography did not include you.

My brain likes to shut down if I ever think on it too much. There is definitely a smack of ancestral guilt in it all. But beyond that, I have a sense much of it synchs with a nauseating and perverse sympathy for Judas that, stuck in the wrong place at the wrong time I could easily cash out on a saviour or likewise have been swept up in any number of heinous social wrongs and have oppressed with the worst of them.

Author, ethicist and theologian Lewis Benedictus Smedes wrote: "The difference between guilt and shame is very clear—in theory. We feel guilty for what we do. We feel shame for what we are" (*Shame and Grace: Healing the Shame We Don't Deserve,* 1994).

Throughout the years I was first, foremost and totally focused on being a street outreach worker. I met more young people and adults navigating the streets than I ever would've imagined possible. Some were long engagements over months, and even years, while others were unanticipated appointments of mere moments. The volatility of any sort of street existence makes it absolutely impossible to anticipate what's next. Or actually—who's next. If nothing else, my book *Bent Hope* is a testimonial to that one intriguing and unnerving reality.

The who's who of the street world is primarily a revolving door of broken-hearted dreamers, survivors and victims. Any broad societal whitewashing that lays claim to something otherwise is simply wrong. Those who speak it out of ignorance are sadly mistaken. Those who speak it with apparent certainty are lying.

To the point—and to be sure that compassionate language or politically correct terminology does not excuse anyone from understanding—every single lazy slob, beggar, crackhead, drunk, hooker, bag lady, mental case and deviant I have known on the streets has revealed themselves at some point as a brokenhearted dreamer, survivor or victim. These are not the rants of a bleeding heart, pie-in-the-sky religious fool. I have plenty of those, but these aren't them. This is simply the truth.

With that said, there is one more truth that remains a mystifying and sad part of the unsung story of the streets. The gravity of relentless shame.

For so many, the back stories should be enough to revoke "shame" as one of the countless burdens to bear. A 16-year-old A-plus student incarcerated for stealing food and clothing, because no adult was providing those for him. An 18-year-old trapped in the sex trade, having been pimped out by her own father since childhood. A 35-year-old career timber logger who lost his hand due to faulty machinery, thus losing his career and ultimately his wife, who did not want to stay with an "unemployed invalid." These are just three of countless single-sentence stories that counter the initial optics, provide vital context, and should be the ultimate levellers on who should and should not be owning the shame.

But that 16-year-old boy was overwhelmed with shame while doing his time. That 18-year-old girl never looked me in the eyes over the several months I knew her. Not once. And that lumberjack's shame festered to a self-loathing and self-destruction like I have never seen before.

And then there was Donald.

His street tenure was 18 hours. Suppertime on a mild Friday evening to noon on Saturday. He wasn't running away so much as being away. He wasn't wandering into the unknown in search of a safe harbour. It was more of an experiment than anything. Zero visual hallmarks of street presence or curb experience. His hair was combed neatly. His clothes were clean. And he had legitimate money in his pocket for snacks, bus fare and even the movies. He was one of the most mild-mannered and polite young people I have ever met in my life. And still, I think his story is crazy.

I met him at hour 17 of his stay on the infamous Yonge Street strip in downtown Toronto. I had seen him sitting on a bench the night before and not given it a second thought. But there he was the next morning, still on the same bench, still in the same clothing. Funny how the uneventfulness of it all made him stand out so dramatically in the midst of the inner-city mayhem. And soon I would find out that it was more than funny. It was painfully ironic.

"Have you been sitting here since last night?" I asked in overstated tones.

"No...Ya...Well, not really...Kinda." His voice grew thinner with each syllable. Stark contrast to the tenor of words I would hear from him next. I told him why I was there, what I did for a living, and dropped a business card between us as instant proof. Immediately, he sat tall, cleared his throat and made sure I did not think he was any kind of street kid.

"No! Oh no! It's not like that!" he declared. "I...I...I...," and once again his voice tapered to near nothing, uncertain of how to continue.

Of all the virtues a street outreach worker has to garner, none is as essential as patience. It took me many long, awkward years to learn this. I was always glad to try and complete unfinished sentences with my best guesses at conversations halted by emotion, fear and uncertainty. And I wasn't very good at it. I would guess I was 50/50 at best at filling in the blanks correctly with my words. Barely a passing grade. But once I learned to let time stand still and wait in silence, I shot up to the honour roll on intuition, reading the signs and body language and understanding that sometimes silence is more telling than words.

In this case, what I knew was what I didn't know. I was stumped during the silence because he was truly unlike any of the others I had known. He didn't rattle like a new runaway. He didn't jangle like a user. He didn't over-project like a rebounder. And he didn't cross his arms or inch away like an abuse survivor. He just sat there, like a nice, shy kid, not sure of what to say.

Why? Because that is exactly who he was.

Once he realized I wasn't going to push him, nor was I going to leave, in his own time he gently spilled the beans. Speaking his own young reality without cursing or cussing. Spending little energy on blame and without contempt. He was just sadly at his wits' end, and these few hours were meant to be his brave notice that he would indeed take a stand and be heard. The problem was that by the time I arrived, he was quite sure he had failed.

Donald was the son of a middle-class family living in the suburbs. The middle brother of three. His school marks were good, but not great. His best marks were in English class because he loved to read. His looks were average. His height was average. He dressed modestly. He had a few friends, but was definitely not popular. He didn't do drugs. Committed no crimes. No foul play. He did not have a girlfriend, but there was a girl at school he really liked who barely even knew his name. He liked sports, but was not very good at them, and was not on any teams.

Just a decent kid, who neither won awards nor made a fuss. A nice boy making his way through the tail end of puberty on the slightly nerdy side. A boy who dreamed big on his own time, but shied away from creating adventure in his day-to-day. A kid you'd see reading at the library or buying a pop at the convenience store and not even think twice about. But these things were not his solace. These things were his pain.

His older brother was a winner on all fronts. An athlete's athlete, a scholar and a teenage heartthrob. His younger brother was a punk and a rebel. A wildcat who partied to excess and caused mayhem wherever he went. As east and west as his brothers were to each other, they did have two momentous things in common—both were incredibly popular in the worlds they chose, and both were hard to ignore from the world Donald watched them from.

And mom and dad knew it no different.

Donald's overnight test from a bench at the hub of Canada's largest city was simply to see if anyone would miss him. No one noticed him when he was there, so he wanted to see if they would when he wasn't. The wealth of mom and dad's parental focus had been spent juggling tournaments and award ceremonies with police conversations and drug interventions. Events soundtracked by either brass marching bands or sweaty speed metal. Lots of fuss at either end. The commotion a parent wishes for and the turmoil they fear. Plenty of both. But none of it included Donald.

As he spoke, he kept checking his cellphone. I didn't need to ask. No one had tried to reach him. The entire experiment was a dud. But it was that fidgeting that revealed evidence of the true trauma in Donald's heart. Only minutes before he departed from my side at the bench, as his arm extended past his sleeve while checking his phone—there they were. Cuts. Not lower wrist cuts in an attempt to end things, but upper forearm slices that occur in the middle of the night in an attempt to feel something. Anything.

Most cutters start in their early teens. Statistically, this form of self-injury is much more prevalent among girls than guys. For some people, cutting actually becomes addictive, and many people continue to cut into adulthood. Thus also spending inordinate amounts of time trying to hide the cuts and come up with cat scratch and rose bush excuses. For some, it's a gateway to other forms of self-injury, such as skin burning with the end of a cigarette or a lit match.

When the subject of cutting first became a teen issue of note, there was a misunderstanding that this was simply a trend among young people with a flair for the dramatic. Punkers and goths and radicals looking to make a statement. All just an eerie part of another scene set against teen angst. Or perhaps occurring under the influence of drugs, intoxication or hallucination.

CHAPTER 13

But time has told a completely different story. For most, it's the loneliest act they will ever know. Far from any group dynamic or adolescent festivity. And most cutters are stone sober when they mark themselves. Certainly sexual, psychological and emotional abuse are often triggers. But for some, they're not even sure why they cut themselves, and that lostness alone becomes spell-binding. And then there are those like Donald. The ones who cut out of neglect. The ones who cut, hoping their pain somehow matters. The ones who cut skin to match the cuts in their soul.

Donald's eyes caught mine as I noticed the fresh scratches on his arm. He yanked his sleeve down, quit speaking and looked away. We sat silently for several minutes. Both simply staring straight ahead. Finally, he stood and tried to look at me. But he couldn't pull off the eye contact, so he looked just above me.

"I gotta go."

Silence.

"I'm so stupid."

Silence.

"I'm so ashamed."

And he was gone.

The good kids. The average kids. The nice kids. The B and C students. The ones void of superstardom. The same ones who will never know that back seat of a police car. They are all around us. Everywhere. Never in the headlines. Not on the evening news. If there is one consistent crime committed by the mainstream in North America, from church picnics to school assemblies to family reunions, it's this: we have forgotten to celebrate them. We have assumed too much from their quiet dispositions and expected too little of their shy wishes. We have painstakingly taught them manners since birth, only to take good behaviour for granted. My entire adult life has been rife with the fringe—experiencing the tough cases and blabbing about the hardcore. And while I believe it has been justified, I do not believe it is the be-all, end-all, or even near to what might really transform the future of my nation. Or any nation.

A good boy sat on a bench with me for an hour. He was neither a big wheel nor a squeaky wheel. Just a normal wheel, ashamed of who he was and what it was doing to him. And that's more than not right. That's abominable. That's a shame!

If you have made it this far into this book, having read the chapters in sequence, you are belly-deep into conversations about people living on the margins of society. I can't guess if you might be intrigued, perplexed, moved or bothered. While I spout off on this and that, indeed, I am suggestive about tweaks we all might consider in our thinking. But ultimately, I am not so full of myself—or anyone else for that matter—that I would outright ask you to actually go and do anything.

Until now.

This is not a request. This is a pleading. I beg you. Go into your day and celebrate the kid in your midst who is simply doing his or her best. If the child is yours to hug, do so simply for being good, and tell them that's why. Have them know you are more than thankful. Have them know you are proud. Live in the sweet moments of the little things, small accomplishments and simple pleasures that keep them well and make them who they are, because at the end of the day, most of us are Donalds on a bench. We're not looking for much, but we do need some.

It's extraordinary what the fruits of the Spirit are not: success, heroics, popularity, good looks, talent, rebellion. "But the fruit of the Spirit is love, joy, peace, patience, kindness, goodness, faithfulness, gentleness and self-control" (Galatians 5:22-23, NIV).

I have no idea where Donald is now, or where his story ends. But I do know we honour him and his story by loving the good kids. Appreciating the nice ones. Enjoying the average ones. And blessing each and every one against shame.

My prayer for Donald would do well on the tailgate of an old two-seater pickup truck:

"No shame."

"Mr. Something."

Amen.

I can't remember that last time I signed up or signed on to anything that turned out as I'd expected or imagined. More often than not, it seems that the tiny print in any contract is in reality the giant sideliner that costs me one or more of the following: more money, more time, more energy, and assuredly, more anxiety. But usually the real problem is that I habitually ignore the small print, putting my faith in the bold headline as though somehow those words mean more than the ones in tiny font.

Foolish.

Maybe we'd all pay closer attention if life itself came with small print attached. How long this bit of joy is guaranteed to last, how much it'll cost to fix that hurt, or how difficult it'll be to get this misunderstanding serviced. If life came with small print like that, we wouldn't make it out of kindergarten before learning to never, ever ignore it.

I have many a spiritually upright friend and associate who would debate with fervour that all the fine print we need is found in Scripture. But I have spent more than enough time in the environs of both faith and folly to know that, while this may be essentially true and is poetic to speak, humanity alone proves it's just not that simple.

But occasionally, a faulty part is warranted longer than the full product. Infrequently, a service representative has the clout to make an exception. And once in a blue moon, the bold print stands alone. Hiccups that surprisingly work in our favour.

Irreverent as it may seem, this is the finest metaphor of all for the ways God has shaken, stirred and poured me out when it's mattered most. Catching me off guard with better than I'd bargained for, while almost always having to override my self-centredness and preconceived expectations in the process.

CHAPTER 14

Heading into my short stint with the International Teams' Christmas excursion for The Romania Project, my mind was tuned to the boldface ABCs:

(A) It's going to be both heart-wrenching and exhausting—I get it.
(B) While I'm part of the volunteer team, doing all the same things as the other volunteers, there will be the added twist for me of simply gigging as Santa at each venue—I get it.
(C) Our goal is to try and bring a bit of Christmas to orphans in Romania, and support and encourage the local volunteers with our efforts—if only conceptually, I get it.

But the banner ABCs of the head never account for the small-print dictionary of the heart. There was no way to prepare for the emotional drop kicks to come. Like looking out the third-storey window of an orphanage in Beclean at an ornate church that had been built using orphans as part of the lug-work labour force. A profoundly backward proposition if there ever was one. Like the visit to a Romanian psychiatric ward added on to the end of our tour, where Santa was bitten three times in an involuntary display of affection by overly jubilant patients. Or, like the sight of a little boy running back to class from a seatless and plumbing-free hole-in-the ground outhouse, 20 yards outside a bleak little schoolhouse filled with unassuming children and a few sweet and sacrificial teachers, in the remarkably impoverished and wintery countryside of Figa.

There are a handful of Hollywood images that North Americans of my vintage remember as darkly iconic from their childhoods, as television gave them a new life away from the theatre. Kids barely old enough to beg their way past bedtime shuddered from behind easy chairs and beneath sofa pillows at the first glimpse of armed primates on horseback chasing humans through cornfields during the original *Planet of the Apes*, the net-wielding child catcher propositioning hidden children with lollipops in *Chitty Chitty Bang Bang*, and of course, the flying monkeys circling the wicked witch of the west in *The Wizard of Oz*. Startling visuals leaving permanent imprints.

For me, that list has always also included one other. Not nearly as graphic, but somehow I was fearfully branded by it all the same. There were the opening scenes of 1971's bizarre and iconic film *Willy Wonka and the Chocolate Factory*, based on Roald Dahl's 1964 novel *Charlie and the Chocolate Factory*, as it imaged four bedridden grandparents living in squalour. It's one of the movie images that rattled me most as a child and has remained vivid in my mind since the very first time I saw it. More than just the staging of what "waiting to die" might look like, it was accented with the uncompromising drama of having it occur in a state of great poverty, heightened by a fate even worse—waiting to die while watching the people around you waiting to die.

Even as a very little boy, when time felt like it would never catch up with me, ultimately these quiet scenes scarred my imagination. Perhaps because even young minds can unknowingly detect what is ultimately fantastical. And more importantly, what isn't.

I'd been at the foot of many a sorrow-filled deathbed for the aged, ill and otherwise. I'd been up close to overwhelming poverty countless times in countless ways. And I'd been tucked in tightly to entire communities of lost hope and shocking despair. But until I arrived in Cluj, I had never seen anything so evocative of all three.

I carried my Santa Claus outfit in a thick garment bag that made it hard to see how many extras accompanied the red ensemble. The team had never seen me in full costume and were unaware that it would take me at least a good 20 minutes to ready myself for full effect, including whitening my eyebrows and rosying my cheeks and nose. I think they may have imagined I was coming with the "Hey, no one else wants to do it" office-party version of Claus. But I had always tried to ramp it up as best I could, remembering my own childhood disappointment with discount mall and school assembly Santas.

While I had explored what I considered Romania's disturbing folklore, unpacking three twisted Santa identities and a series of creepy antics, I came with my fingers crossed, willing to trust the better judgment of whoever was in charge at any given time, from venue to venue. And while I tried not to overthink or expect too much philosophically, I did make a few small practical assumptions. One of them simply being that there would always be someplace I could change in and out of my outfit.

Unlike with the orphanages, when we visited adult facilities, there was no formal program attached to it. Visiting was the program. Thus, when we arrived at the elderly care centre, the first order of business as far as I was concerned was getting me changed. Our team entered a narrow entrance into a long hallway as various staff members looked on suspiciously. Two or three people began asking questions and giving instructions in Romanian as our local volunteers worked to interpret and help sort out some of the confusion about our presence and who had okayed us being there in the first place. Somewhere in the midst of all the confusion, I was loosely directed to a bathroom down the hall, and told to hurry up and change while things got sorted out. I wandered away on my own, feeling duly awkward as a few slow-moving residents and cross-armed staff members warily eyeballed me.

While it may not be the norm, it's also not radically uncommon to find an awkward dynamic between people who have come to serve from wealthy nations and the people who are engaged in the gruelling day-to-day realities at hand. Mistrust, pride, hesitant thanksgiving—and sometimes even green envy—are a motley crew of sentiments to temper simultaneously when you represent the receiving side of things. It's hard enough to make your own way through the melee, without the distraction of buffering outside parties you aren't sure won't ultimately make things worse. It's not unlike what I've known so well during my entire adult outreach career. I have stood the middle ground and guessed my way through it a million times, having hosted street walks for corporate executives and political leaders who want an up-close look at homelessness before heading home, media people willing to trade profile for an angle, and church groups who want to serve the poor as a Friday night outing. There's something right and something wrong with it all, all at the same time. I've been there when it's gone well. I've been there when it's gone nowhere. And I've been there when it's been a disaster. And I know one thing for sure. If I were on the nursing staff of one of the most despairing old age facilities in all of Europe, in a country barely poking its head out from decades of tyranny and anguish, and I saw a bunch of wide-eyed, blue-jeaned and wind-breakered Canadians walk in carrying pieces of fruit and jingle bells, I'm quite sure I'd have lots to mumble and chirp about too.

I kept my head low and ducked into the room I thought I'd been waved toward. No sooner had the door shut behind me than I looked up to see and know that I would go down in history as one of the most disturbing Santa impersonators of all time. I had stepped into an unlocked women's bathroom stall, where a roly little toothless babushka of a woman was perched with her skirt around her ankles. She croaked all kinds of Romanian expletives at me as I darted back into the hall, scurried out the side door, and hid inside the team van. Merry Christmas. Ugh.

Unsure of what else to do, but positive that returning in anything but a disguise would only make things worse, and knowing the team had already abandoned the foyer and had begun going room to room, I decided to change right then and there in the clear-windowed van, in broad daylight. As I attempted to sink low between the seats, I did what I always do when my mind is spinning—talk out loud to myself, God, and whoever else comes to mind.

"Way to go, Tim. Great start, you fool! Aaaw God, c'mon, I'm really trying here! Okay, okay lady, I am so sorry. I so didn't mean to freak you out! Please, please, no one walk by, ah please!"

I changed like a panicking criminal late for a heist, slid the van door open, jumped out and tried to bounce everything into place. Just as I'd finished straightening my beard in the exterior driver-side mirror, the side door of the elderly care centre swung open. It was the little woman to whom I had inadvertently made my first visit. She hiked past me carrying an old mop and bucket, murmuring a blue streak while staring me down. This encounter allowed me the time and composure to note some probable mental challenges, and guess that she was some kind of in-house worker or volunteer who had simply taken a latrine break when I, um, made her acquaintance. I couldn't tell if she was glaring at, and talking her way through, the ridiculous sight of Santa haplessly standing all alone in the driveway, trying to figure out if I was real or in her imagination, or if she had x-ray vision and knew I was the guy who stepped in on her in the loo. Regardless, she went about her business, unimpressed by whatever I was or was not.

Eventually, I made my way to the side entrance and peered through the door. Our team leader, Bob, spotted me, rushed me down the hall while listening to the ten-second version of the story, burst into laughter, and bumped me into the first room of seniors while dubbing me "Bad Santa."

But that was to be the last of the laughs on this day. Instead, there would follow incomprehension, bewilderment and heart-rending surprises.

The team had been divided into two groups so as not to overwhelm and to be sure sufficient time was spent visiting each room. We were not permitted to bring gifts or in any way be loud or disturbing. The game plan was executed as it had been agreed on. Each group of five or six from our team would enter a room that housed anywhere from six to 14 occupied beds, greet anyone who was awake and seemed accepting of our unfamiliar presence, and simply try and sit at their side or take their hand. The only things we were permitted to bring as a gesture of gifting were bananas. Fresh fruit was a luxury and most of the seniors were so fragile that anything as hard as an apple was too difficult to tackle. But a peeled banana is 75 per cent water and 25 per cent dry matter, and an ideal treat. And so, as oddly token as it seemed, our Christmas bananas were received as small treasures. Thus, our small teams would move from bed to bed, placing fruit grown in some beautiful far-far-away tropical locale into the withered and twisted hands of a forgotten few stuck in the un-sunniest setting imaginable.

One hundred and twenty residents, living out their final years, months, days and moments as the ultimate throw-away casualties of war. Literal wars of bombs, bullets and human carnage they had remarkably survived. Figurative and relentless wars of the psyche, ravaged by poverty and survival of the fittest, if not the luckiest. Emotional wars waged by stark reality attacking tender memories. And relentless battles of the soul. Hearts and minds wondering if—and why—God had abandoned them.

Cold, dank and grey, the atmosphere was permissive of nothing more than grief, as far as I was concerned. The very first thing that popped into my mind the moment I peered into the first room I visited was that chilling opening grandparent scene from Willy Wonka, where long lives had been reduced to a nothing-left-but-to-die existence. Face-to-face with one of my earliest childhood fears.

A wobbly few eked their way from their rooms to the dimly lit hallways, set apart from the immobile majority. Toques, scarves and threadbare shawls were common accessories to standard bedwear, as winter pressed hard against the overwhelming lack of provisions. The toxic odour of gangrene combined with the septic pong of dysentery wafted through the hallways. Hacking coughs and incoherent cries for help kept under-resourced staff on a slow and steady pace of hands-on care and hands-off self-preservation.

And then there was Santa. In the midst of the unthinkable came the ridiculous. I stood at the doorway of the first room I was to visit and felt overwhelmed in a way I had never known. Shockingly and strangely embarrassed, to the nth degree, even though I was completely unidentifiable and did not know a soul. Terrified by the knowledge that a Santa visit had never been attempted here. Too researched and schooled for my own good in a ludicrous and dark Santa lore that Romanian seniors, if no one else, might know. And literally sick to my stomach that at any moment prior to this, I had humiliatingly thought I had something significant to offer. If I had owned any supernatural Santa magic in that moment, I would surely have used it all to make myself vanish.

But God would have none of it. He had not brought me this far, to this preposterous a moment, so that I would vanish, bail or bargain my way out of it. But rather that He would do more than teach me humility on this day; He would wrap me in it and make me wear it. That He would do more than school me in the counting of blessings; He would overwhelm me with the mathematics. That He would not just have me face my little boy fears; He would make me own them. And that while I have never—and may never—conquer them, in the end I would be left with no other conceivable mortal, or immortal, alternative but to bring them to Him.

My actual Santa task, while weathering to my soul in ways I could not fathom, was quite simple in nature. I moved across the hallways at intervals double the pace of each team, so that I could be present for the second half of each team encounter in each room. This meant I arrived in any given room just after the surprise of wandering banana-bearing guests had settled.

The range of responses was radical in its extremes. From invalid patients anxiously trying to crawl through bed rails to reach for my hand as I walked by, to surly residents who would open one eye to see what the commotion was, and close it instantly without a second thought or any remote interest. From physically incapacitated seniors turning purple with shock— leaving me to wonder if it was joy or terror—to the mentally incapacitated who were clearly perplexed, left to wonder if I was truly present in the room or merely in their minds.

One frail old soul, just well enough to make her way to the hallway, saw me coming and frantically scooted behind a staff member, shrieking and weeping. Whoever she imagined me to be—Claus from ancient Romanian lore, or some bright variance of the grim reaper—the worker translated her cries that she believed I had come to take her to her grave.

Knowing my place in the great Santa charade has never come easy. While I have always enjoyed hamming it up with my buddies, my personal interests in being part of the thespian trade have been nil. But ultimately, a decent Santa routine requires some commitment to acting. Somehow, what started as simply wanting my own little girl and boy to spot Saint Nick frolicking in their backyard had unexpectedly evolved into an actual December role. Better still, and more complex, several roles.

Backyard Santa is the simplest. Playful, silly, elf-like. And never close enough to be debunked.

Mindless celebration. Innocent and daft.

Group home and hospital Santa came along as one request simply followed the next. A live-and-learn process, this Claus just plays it as he sees it. Jolly when it's right, gentle when it's due. And somewhat bashful up close, fearful of the obvious giveaways.

Mindful celebration. Discerning and attentive.

And if it wasn't already biting off more than you could chew for a non-actor to step into these arenas, the guise of Santa Claus at an impoverished Romanian elderly care centre sure was. For it was there that my shtick wasn't enough. It was there that I was pressed to do more than pretend and play make-believe. It was there that I felt no other alternative than to assume my greatest role. It was there that I was truly an imposter.

Mind-numbing celebration. Perplexing and improbable.

CHAPTER 14

While minds and memories in various states of wellness processed the absurd first of a Santa in their midst, a startling portion of the pained population responded as though a true holy man had miraculously arrived. More than a dozen times, tears began to roll as I drew near to the bedsides of those with outstretched hands. Once there, with whatever strength they possessed, they would kiss my hands, pull me as close as possible, and weep with words that our Romanian volunteers translated into pleas for healing and to be taken away.

Drawn inches from their faces, I looked down into blood-streaked eyes, stained faces, toothless mouths, and chins covered in drool. The stench of empty stomachs escaped in their breathing and the saliva of desperate appeals was uncontrollably spat in my face. All of it as close as a human being could ever be to his or her greatest childhood fear. A place I had always, and only, anticipated horror would loom.

The very place God appeared.

After 40-plus years of knowing Christian tradition well, decades of involvement in church activity and service, and a quarter of a century awkwardly navigating my way through my own personal faith commitment, it was as an imposter among a group of decaying and dying people whom I couldn't understand that I received celebration like I had never known it.

Sacred celebration. Outrageous and breathtaking.

While in each room, after gentle greetings were made and tropical fruits were distributed, each team would take the time to softly sing two or three Christmas carols before moving on. Usually timing had it that Santa appeared just around when the first carol began. As the team sang, Santa moved slowly through the room.

After three or four room visits, anxiety gave way to loose expectations. I expected some people to adore the imposter, some to go along, some to be bewildered and some to ignore him. And I expected the team to create a sweet tone in the unlikeliest of places by the time I had arrived.

I did not expect there would be more fine print than I had already been wonderfully damaged by.

But a room with seven beds for fallen saints and one for the unlikeliest of life-givers was still in store.

Halfway through our rounds, with our team in a lovely tender groove, I found myself sitting at the bedside of a frail old man with gauze and padding covering half his face, while he held my index finger in his shrunken hand. The team sang softly. While we did not know the carols in Romanian, we chose ones that were centuries old and would carry melodies known around the world. In each room, we completed our visit with "Silent Night," just as we would in this room of eight. And in each room, inevitably the moaning and upset would ease as residents joined in, in their own language or humming along. Those precious moments were—and still are—indescribable. Grief-filled with the gravity of death itself, and glorious with the light of God, all at once. But in this room, for these moments, it was even more than that.

Lying directly across from me was an old man who paid no mind to the kerfuffle we caused. He didn't budge, he didn't strain to see who we were or comprehend why we were there, and he had no intrigue for the red imposter well within his sightline. He lay motionless as one of our team members put a banana on his rickety bedside stand, gently rubbed his arm, and moved away. I watched him sadly, knowing he knew what I knew. We could not and would not fix a thing.

Our time in this room of eight was drawing to a close, so the team began to sing "Silent Night." Gently, warmly, with team members holding the hands or rubbing the arms of the seven respondents. We weren't more than two or three lines into the carol when the old loner began to squirm. He drew his skeletal arms from beneath the blankets and struggled from his right side to his left. Finally propping himself onto his left elbow, he agonizingly reached toward his tiny bedside stand.

I rose to my feet, took the few paces that separated us, and sat on the edge of his bed. By this time, he had jimmied the little drawer open just far enough that his fingertips could reach inside. Inches off the mark, with no strength left, he paused, stuck in place. But his eyes were wide with ambition. As he caught his breath, I shimmied the drawer open until his hand dropped inside. Unable to sit high enough to look in, his wiry hand scrambled through the ancient odds and ends that were kept there. He worked his way through the final few touchstones of a long life all but forgotten—yellowed envelopes, handwritten notes and few tiny mementos of tender moments and victories past. With a final strain, his hand made its way to the very backside of that drawer, to gather up an item he knew was there, but that had been relegated to the rear, having had no contemporary purpose in his world.

And with a giant sigh, he lifted his hand victoriously to reveal a harmonica. A free-reed instrument known best for its distinctly flavoured sound in American blues, folk and country music. Perhaps the last of all things I might have guessed would magically appear in his grip.

Adrenalized by the sight and feel of this unlikely old friend, he nodded at my arm, prompting me to help him wiggle into an upright position. Which I did.

CHAPTER 14

The team kept singing, nuanced by the sounds of shared hums emanating from the beds. But all eyes were on the old man. I pressed my arm on his back to keep him propped upright and could feel his ribs poking through his layered clothing. And once in place, having gathered his breath and mustered his strength, he exhaled into improbable song. His puckered lungs were renewed, his tone was rich, and the dusty melody of candlelight piercing through blackness filled the air. From the last place on earth I would ever seek it came the unconscionable sound of abundant life.

And as he quickly regained his feel for vibrato and the bending of notes, our singing faded until we all sat silent, and simply listened. And every eye found a tear. Too astounding, too implausible, too beautiful to believe that even heaven's angels did not quiet their harps to listen.

Penned by Father Joseph Mohr in 1816, and set to melody by musician/school teacher Franz Xavier Gruber on Christmas Eve 1818, the dots connecting "Silent Night" to these special moments in Romania are ironic to say the least. Mohr and Gruber created the lyrics and melody in Oberndorf, Austria (less than 900 kilometres from Cluj, Romania), and it was first performed at midnight mass at Nikolaus-Kirche (Church of St. Nicholas). It is also intriguing that the music for "Silent Night" was written for guitar, rather than organ, which was very rare for church music. Indeed, I would have to believe there was no comprehension at all that it would ever find exorbitant beauty by way of the unimagined harmonica. Still, connecting just one more set of unlikely dots through history is that nearby Austria, where "Silent Night" was both written and first performed, became the centre of worldwide harmonica production less than two decades after the carol was written and shared. Incongruent facts, except for this story.

As his final note faded, his body dropped. I could feel the release as he deflated and slid back into his pillow. *"Multumesc, multumesc,"* ("Thank you, thank you") Santa whispered in his ear, as the old man shrugged his way back to his starting point on his right side, returning to his distant presence. As he had no strength for words or gumption for anything more than a glassy-eyed stare, we left him in peace and exited, knowing we had received an unprecedented gift.

Why? Why would a man in his state dig into his final reserves to shock those who could in no way resolve his dilemma, by sharing the hidden beauty of combined talent and emotion torn from the early pages of his life story?

Perhaps "Why" is the wrong question.

How?

How did a man with nothing left to live for find it in his soul to devastate a group of strangers and his sorrowful peers with a gift consuming more energy than his body might bear?

Mary. The only sensible or comprehensible answer for both "Why" and "How" I can think of is Mary, the mother of Jesus.

We Baptist boys aren't generally schooled in what to really make of Mary's glorious role in Scripture. By and large, we've counted on cautious acceptance of the noncontroversial this-and-thats our Catholic friends have shared with us and silver screen movies distort to keep her conveniently packaged for our theological consumption.

But here in the no-one-knows-ness of a forgotten few, the celebration of Mary's inspiration rings only too loud and clear.

In the New Testament's book of Luke, Joseph, Mary and the baby Jesus were visited by shepherds who shared the message they'd been given by a host of angels, that a "Saviour" had been born, and while all they told were amazed, "Mary treasured up all these things and pondered them in her heart" (Luke 2:19, NIV).

Later in the same book of Luke, Jesus at age 12 went missing. When Joseph and Mary found Him in the temple courts in Jerusalem, after three days of searching anxiously, He responded with words no human would ever anticipate—"Didn't you know I had to be in my Father's house?" And while perplexed, even still, Mary "treasured all these things in her heart" (Luke 2:49-51, NIV).

Treasuring—keeping, guarding, watching over. Intensified in translation with two compound formations to mean joyful receiving, careful keeping and profound valuing.

What had the old man "treasured" in his heart? Places, faces, moments, conversations, voices, sights, sounds? Beyond the despair, disappointment, sacrifice and fatigue of a life set to end unceremoniously, and all but alone. And still fuelled to the bitter end with the know-how of returning to the treasure, digging it up and sharing its splendour? What spark of joy was he still able to set aflame? What memory of music and celebration spun unannounced in the centre of his heart?

I have filled my heart with a great many things thus far. But filling your heart is a complex matter. For more than love is anxious to reside there. Sorrow, guilt, shame, envy and anger have always found ways to bully their way in.

What I had not done was make a covenant to "treasure" God's gifts in my heart. To fill a wellspring in my soul that would allow me to receive life and give life even in my darkest hour. Not until I was guided by the frailest of the frail while in my grandest state of imposter.

CHAPTER 14

At last, good, good news in the fine print.

(Lyrics from "God Knows," from the album *Under the Red Sky*, 1990, written by Bob Dylan—world-famous singer, songwriter, poet—and harmonica enthusiast)

God knows that when you see it
God knows you've got to weep
God knows the secrets of your heart
He'll tell them to you when you're asleep.

God knows there's a river
God knows how to make it flow
God knows you ain't gonna be taking
Nothing with you when you go.

God knows there's a purpose
God knows there's a chance
God knows you can rise above the darkest hour
Of any circumstance.

The first time I met Horace, it was from two metres behind his backside, while he lay on the ground with his face in the garden. I was receiving my round of introductions to a new group home placement, as my staff escort walked me to the patio. Horace's head and shoulders were as lost in the foliage as were his attention and imagination. While sweetly reprimanded and failingly coaxed to arise and greet me like a gentleman, Horace was far too gone to another world to pay any mind. He just stayed on his tummy, giggling in the flora.

"Eeeew! Bunderful! Bunderful!"

He repeated himself over and over, pausing only for snickers of joy.

"Horace, *please.*" The admonishing grew stricter.

But he would have none of it, and heard none of it. For there was something far too consuming and amusing stealing him away.

"Eeeew, so bunderful! Really bunderful!"

Finally, the staff host stepped from the patio and gently shook Horace by the shoulders. "Horace, there is someone new to meet. Please stand up."

Horace seemed startled by the interruption of her voice, tugging him away from his enchantment in the garden. He had not meant to be rude or stubborn. He was simply being Horace.

To slide back from the flowers, prop himself on his knees and finally stand upright took some serious time, energy and focus. But stand he did. Horace was a heavy-set young man with Down syndrome, a wide crack-lipped smile and the thickest pop-bottle glasses I had ever seen. Yet, even once on his feet, he had not left his sense of intrigue behind. Nor could he, because the hub of his focus had come along for the ride.

Horace stood directly in front of me and gleefully continued, "Bunderful! Eeeew, bunderful!"

There, sitting on the nose of his giant glasses, was a tiny green inchworm.

A fascinating creature mere mortals would've missed, or dismissed, filling Horace with a delight too wonderful—nay, too "bunderful"—to miss.

It would take no imagination to guess, having made it now to the end of this book, at the metaphors and parallels I might choose to draw between Horace's delight in an inchworm and God's delight in you. That even among the splendid beauty of brilliant petals and ripened leaves, and a population fronted by magnificent butterflies and robust bumble bees, a tiny inchworm is deemed too wonderful to overlook or miss celebrating. But real life does not wait on the sentimental words found in poems, songs, or the tender conclusions in book epilogues. The real matter is in believing it is so, and living as such, as you enter a garden that also includes overwhelming weeds, unsightly fungus and ravenous predators.

Many of the greatest oppressors in history were those who spiritualized, and over-spiritualized, every little thing and purposed every moment to suit their own existence. At the other extreme have been those who have mistaken humility with emptiness.

But even spiritual skeptics might agree that Horace had an innate and admirable sense of priority.

The famed satirical novelist Kurt Vonnegut Jr. (often self-described as a humanist, agnostic and atheist) once said: "Enjoy the little things in life, for one day you'll look back and realize they were big things."

Therein lies the great dilemma, somewhere past the overlapping filters that too often retain our souls: We think ourselves too little. We think others too little. We think God too little.

We enjoy so little.

It's a mad thing that we would strive for so much and enjoy so little. What is it that keeps us from absorbing the very fullness of knowing how to give and receive joy, to enter joy, to enjoy?

The nuanced answers are surely as uniquely skewed as each of our own identities. But I would imagine that the core issues are likely a small and consistent few: identity, regret, fear, envy, pride, entitlement. The fullness of enjoyment comes not in simply giving or receiving joy, but in the willingness and desire to participate in both.

Entitlement—among humankind's slyest foes—is a prime example of enjoyment gone wrong. This polluted form of enjoyment negates the fullness and richness of its true meaning. History is rife with examples of oppression caused by the self-serving notion of entitlement. Receiving satisfaction by costing others of it, and believing it rightfully so.

There is no true peace in it, and it ultimately contradicts belonging. Few, if any, could phrase it as simply and profoundly as Mother Teresa:

"If we have no peace, it is because we have forgotten that we belong to each other."

Inchworms are no more innocent in their domain than humans are in theirs. Gardeners and farmers would testify that most species of inchworms have voracious appetites and are able to nosh their way through entire crops. The truth is outside of the world of children's songs and cartoons, inchworms are considered pests. And still, but for the garden and field, where else could they belong? While we are no more inchworm than Horace is God, the truth remains: there is beauty, value and intrigue to behold in each one of us. The pests, the cocooned and the pollinators alike. But unlike bugs, or any other creature on earth, we can choose to celebrate one another. In doing so, we bring out the best in each other and create a garden akin to the garden of God's first design, where everyone belongs, and for everyone to enjoy. Imagining it as no less than "on earth as it is in heaven."

If you've come this far, chapter by chapter, you've met many of my friends and teachers. You've perhaps laughed with my acquaintances and cried for complete strangers. Names and pseudonyms aside, if I have any small portion right, my prayer is that you've found some semblance of yourself within these pages. And in that, that you know you belong. That you are worthy to be celebrated.

There is a strange dynamic in the writing process that includes equal parts self-doubt and enthusiasm, pride and humility, shame and encouragement. I've been tripped by one and lifted by the other repeatedly, only to find myself no less self-conscious about my own brokenness and hypocrisy. I'm compelled then to thank you for generously travelling these pages with me, and to ask your forgiveness for the unavoidable self-indulgence inherent in writing in this manner.

And in conclusion, allow me to take you just one step further with me on this bumpy adventure, with a glorious challenge set against side-stepping those we might consider awkward, eerie, unfamiliar, unknown and perhaps downright strange (root of the word "stranger").

Eighteen words from the New Testament that splendidly sum up the several thousand I threw at you. Hebrews 13:2 is a stunning and mystical verse of scripture that all on its own would change this world forever, if we truly pursued it: "Do not forget to entertain strangers, for by so doing some people have entertained angels without knowing it" (NIV).

Various translations substitute "entertain" with "be kind to," "be gracious to" and "show love to."

Epilogue

What a world we would find! What a garden of grandeur we would discover! What adventure we'd gain! What peace would overcome! And what heavenly belonging we would know!

Every single one of us.

Bunderful.

Benediction By Sister Sue Mosteller, C.S.J.

How Do I Listen?

How
Do I
Listen to others?
As if everyone were my Master
Speaking to me
His
Cherished
Last
Words.

Hafiz. *The Gift: Poems by Hafiz the Great Sufi Master.* Translated by
Daniel Ladinsky. New York: Penguin Putnam Inc., 1999.

Tim's stories mirror for us what the poet Hafiz describes. Tim hears and
sees the Master when Gramma Lu convinces little Bronty that God made him
special and when the hacking beggar woman spends her precious "take for the
day" to buy chicken and noodles for the homeless war veteran. Tim sees—and
hears—his Master's precious last words: "It is accomplished." And so it is that
Tim's encounters are really blessings—for him, for the marginalized ones, and
for you and I. He recognizes and is enlightened by various and sundry expressions of the Master's cherished last words.

Thus, the book in itself *is* the benediction! It is Good News, the gospel message, the Word that brings hope. It is saying (*dicere*) good things (*bene*), just as
Jesus did when He announced, "Blessed are the poor" and walked with the
street people of His day.

The apostles didn't get it. We don't get it. But in raspy voices Tim hears precious words, and in fearful behaviours he connects with radiant hearts. And he has the nerve to be poor enough himself to approach our most impoverished members to receive their blessing! Yes, he dares to allow the most unlikely in our world to announce Good News to him—which he, in turn, announces to us—in the hope that we will finally get it. Dancing with dynamite, indeed!

I love this book because it touches me and blesses me in my secret passion to become a *true* disciple. It challenges me and calls me, not so much to join Tim on the streets at night, but to listen for the Master's voice in everyone in *my* daily life, convinced of the hidden blessing waiting to be given me. It prompts me to see my people with my heart focused on the precious, vulnerable, often broken heart, like mine, that silently beats below the behaviour and the appearance.

Jean Vanier, my friend and my brother in spirit, has so often commented that Jesus did not say, "Blessed are those who care for the poor," but "Blessed *are* the poor." In all our efforts to help others and to express our deep compassion, however, the key is to do so with the conviction that God's blessing is coming to us directly from the ones we serve.

So you and I have only to be empty and poor enough to listen to everyone around us in our lives today. In our presence to each one, we—like Tim—will tune our inner ear to recognize the still, small voice of the Beloved blessing us. We see and hear God in Jesus, but we also see and hear the Master in the voice of a suffering sister or brother.

Each one of us so much needs to be blessed. Tim's friends and our colleagues may be our unlikely ministers in spirit. They bless us with their incredible depth, generosity, courage, openness, truth and spirit. It is for you and I to finally surrender to the message Jesus so wants us to comprehend. He's hiding in His "blessed" ones, waiting to be merciful to us and to speak into our hearts His cherished last words.

Sister Sue Mosteller, C.S.J.

Born in Ohio, Sue Mosteller received most of her education from the Sisters of St. Joseph in Toronto. She entered the congregation of St. Joseph after high school, and as a sister taught school in B.C. and Ontario for 15 years, during which time she completed her degree in English at the University of Toronto. In 1967, she met Jean Vanier, who called her to organize and preach Faith and Sharing retreats in Canada and abroad. Inspired by Vanier, Sue became interested in the plight of persons with a disability, and organized a Faith and Light pilgrimage to Lourdes in 1971.

From there, Sue moved to the L'Arche Daybreak community in Richmond Hill, Ontario, where she has lived and worked with people with disabilities for more than 30 years. Sue replaced Jean Vanier as the international coordinator of L'Arche and travelled widely, visiting and assisting in birthing new L'Arche communities in many countries. With Father Henri J.M. Nouwen, Sue opened the Dayspring, a small centre for spiritual growth that offers retreats and workshops focusing on spiritual life, and announcing a spiritual life inspired by the poor at the heart of the community. Her most recent book is entitled Light Through the Crack: Life After Loss.

When Henri Nouwen died in 1996, Sue was named executrix of his literary estate. She is presently retired at L'Arche Daybreak, where she works with the published and unpublished legacy of Henri Nouwen.

Tim Huff

Tim Huff was born, raised and continues to make his home in Toronto, Canada. Tim, married to Diane since 1987, is the father of two children—Sarah Jane and Jake.

At age 16, Tim volunteered at The Ontario Camp of the Deaf for a summer. While unexpected at the time, this opportunity in his younger years was extremely pivotal in shaping the direction of his life. Tim learned sign language and served at the camp for 15 summers—the first five as a counsellor through summer high school and college breaks, and the following ten as the camp's staff director, through a Youth Unlimited (Toronto YFC) summer partnership.

In his late teens, after a year of formal studies in classic animation at Sheridan College, Tim decided on a substantial change in direction and completed a two-year Humber College course, receiving a developmental service worker honours diploma. During that time, and for the two years that followed, Tim served in paid and volunteer positions in several residential and institutional settings.

Throughout Tim's youth, the rock band he fronted (Double Edge) performed in youth detention centres, halfway houses, community centres and for charity events in an effort to bring messages of hope through contemporary music. It was there that Tim sensed a calling to work among what at the time were called "troubled" youth. (Tim continues in music to this day as the lead singer for the band Outrider, performing in a myriad of venues, including bars, biker rallies, street festivals, and for fund and awareness raising events in support of charitable causes.)

In 1987, Tim began full-time work with Youth Unlimited (Toronto YFC), the Toronto chapter of an international Christian agency committed to helping young people develop holistically, both personally and spiritually, by providing caring people to whom they can turn. Over the next 23 years, Tim would have the opportunity to—as he puts it—"learn, grow, lead, struggle, succeed, fail, fail again, find astounding joy, know unbearable grief, and be ridiculously humbled on a journey that I could never have imagined."

At age 23, Tim became the founder and director of Frontlines Youth Centre in Toronto's northwest end. After four years of leadership at Frontlines, Tim pursued a two-year transition plan that would allow him to follow his interests into Canada's largest inner city, while training the incoming director. For the following eight years, Tim worked directly on the streets with homeless youth and adults, committed to being present among the "hidden" homeless—primarily youth so broken by sexual and physical abuse that they would not leave the street to enter any building or facility for help. His outreach had him in alleyways, under bridges and on the streets daily for nearly a decade.

During that time, Tim became a prominent public speaker, advocating for the broad necessity of an appropriate social-justice response to domestic poverty and homelessness.

Over that same time, through Youth Unlimited, Tim also developed Toronto's "Operation Good Thing" campaign—a Christmas season street-relief program that has drawn thousands of people into participation and sacrificial giving on behalf of the poor, and includes the partnerships of ten inner-city agencies invested in practically and relationally reaching out to homeless people of all ages.

In 2001, Tim designed a new outreach program for and with Youth Unlimited, called "Light Patrol." As its director, he established this specialized street outreach with a commitment to caring for the long-term and immediate needs of homeless youth and young adults. Under Tim's leadership, street out-reach workers (staff and volunteers) were trained and sent out in teams to build safe relationships with youth, rebuild trust, and move young people into healthy adulthood. Since its inception, under Tim's leadership, the Light Patrol outreach expanded to include a street medical outreach called "Health Light" and a uniquely focused outreach among teenagers and young adults involved, or at risk of involvement, in the sex trade, called "Safe Light."

Tim has also been an active member of the National Roundtable on Poverty and Homelessness, since 2003, which has included a specific role as chair for national Street Level conferences in Ottawa, drawing together leaders and front line workers from across Canada for training, equipping, networking and encouragement, and dialoguing with all levels of government regarding domestic poverty.

Tim served for several years on the board of directors for the Daily Bread Food Bank, one of Canada's most acclaimed hunger reduction agencies. Tim currently sits on the board of directors for Hockey for the Homeless as its director of outreach. Hockey for the Homeless is a national charity that integrates the corporate world and the professional and amateur hockey world to assist agencies serving among Canada's homeless population.

Since the turn of the millennium, Tim has travelled extensively throughout Canada and the United States and into several countries around the world, researching, networking, training, and encouraging others around proactive measures and compassionate responses to poverty and homelessness. He has been an active public speaker across North America around issues of contemporary social justice, faith-based responsibility and opportunity, domestic poverty, hope, dignity and street culture, speaking in schools (elementary to post-secondary), churches, and in corporate and government settings.

Tim wrote and illustrated a best-selling, award-winning children's book (and teaching guide) regarding homelessness called *The Cardboard Shack Beneath the Bridge: Helping Children Understand Homelessness.* It was released in bookstores throughout North America in April 2007, published by Castle Quay Books, with a foreword by The Honourable Hilary M. Weston.

His second book, for adults and teens, called *Bent Hope: A Street Journal* (also published by Castle Quay Books), was released in 2008 and has also gone on to be an award winner and best-seller. It is an exposé of more than 20 years of stories from the street and the relevant implications of Christian faith and social justice. This book includes a foreword by international best-selling author Michael Frost and a benediction by Canadian multi-award-winning singer-songwriter Steve Bell.

The release of *Dancing with Dynamite: Celebrating Against the Odds* also marks the introduction of Tim's next adventure—the Hope Exchange.

The Hope Exchange's national vision is to inspire individuals and families to invest time and care in the lives of broken-hearted people in their midst, to encourage and come alongside staff and volunteers who serve in the areas of front line care among marginalized people groups and those invested in the education and well-being of children, and to facilitate relevant and purposeful social-justice conversations in academic, faith-based and corporate settings. The Hope Exchange endeavours to provide a humble, well-informed and well-networked voice of practical experience and contemporary advocacy around issues of domestic poverty, faith-conscious expressions of benevolence and compassionate community development. It aims to gather together like-minded people from a range of walks and professions, united by the gravity of knowing and sharing in the complex hurt of hope, the anticipation of hope, and hope realized with—and for—all people.

Bringing hope to hopegivers, challenging all people to serve well, and inspiring individuals to celebrate one another.

Objective One: Bringing hope to the hopegivers.

Various adaptations of the term "caregiver" have been, and are, used to describe a great many people simply by way of profession—nurses, developmental service workers, those who serve among the poor, etc. The list goes on to include similar notions among school teachers and others who have children and/or adults in their care. But too often these great callings are diminished by generalizations and descriptors that essentially, and sometimes ultimately, focus on tasks rather than their greatest core value. Instead, I believe that all caregivers and educators are at their best when they are esteemed as—and serve as—"hopegivers" inside the arena of their position's associated tasks and charges.

Of course, most people enter these kinds of roles as professionals and volunteers alike, with a passion to care for, equip and inspire others thoughtfully, tenderly and selflessly. But emotional, physical, mental, and spiritual fatigue often become commonplace due to a shortage—or absence of—resources, encouragement and support.

The Hope Exchange strives to find meaningful and creative ways to honour, encourage, inspire and come alongside the hopegivers.

Objective Two: Challenging all people to serve well.

The heartbeat of this challenge is a simple but profound truth—people are at their best when they serve well, both in what they give, and in what they receive. Sadly, the contemporary challenges and distractions of North American society have stolen greatly from the mainstream's prioritization and/or availability to serve. Charitably, voluntarily, unselfishly and faithfully, too few people serve. And even fewer serve *well*.

The Hope Exchange, via partnerships and its own initiatives, strives to identify and provide opportunities for people to truly serve well by coming alongside others who desire the same—thereby being at their best while and because they are giving their best.

Objective Three: Inspiring individuals to celebrate one another.

Every generation, from every civilization throughout the history of humankind, has been called upon to see its way clear through competing messages about what to seek out, strive for and attain. At no time has it been more difficult to process opposing influences than now. And nowhere is that discussion more complex than in *what,* and more importantly *who,* you choose to celebrate, why and how.

The Hope Exchange strives to model celebration in all its endeavours as a vital component of nurturing.

www.thehopeexchange.ca

CASTLE QUAY BOOKS

For more information and to explore the rest of our titles visit
www.castlequaybooks.com